THE
30-MINUTE
MILLIONAIRE

THE
30-MINUTE
MILLIONAIRE

THE SMART WAY TO ACHIEVING
FINANCIAL FREEDOM

PETER J. TANOUS
JEFF COX

Humanix Books
www.humanixbooks.com

Humanix Books

The 30-Minute Millionaire
Copyright © 2016 by Peter J. Tanous and Jeff Cox
All rights reserved

Humanix Books, P.O. Box 20989, West Palm Beach, FL 33416, USA
www.humanixbooks.com | info@humanixbooks.com

Library of Congress Cataloging-in-Publication Data

Tanous, Peter J., author.
  The 30-minute millionaire / by Peter J. Tanous & Jeff Cox.
    pages cm
  Includes bibliographical references and index.
  ISBN 978-1-63006-039-8 (hardcover : alk. paper)
1. Investments. 2. Finance, Personal. I. Title.
  HG4521.T3177 2016
  332.024'01--dc23
                        2015031266

Interior Design: Ben Davis

Humanix Books is a division of Humanix Publishing, LLC. Its trademark, consisting of the words "Humanix" is registered in the Patent and Trademark Office and in other countries.

Disclaimer: The information presented in this book is meant to be used for general resource purposes only; it is not intended as specific financial advice for any individual and should not substitute financial advice from a finance professional.

ISBN: 978-1-63006-039-8 (Hardcover)
ISBN: 978-1-63006-040-4 (E-book)

Printed in the United States of America

Contents

Acknowledgments

In any book project, there are many people who contribute to the final product besides the names who appear on the cover. Thanks first to Debby Englander, our editor, for her sound editorial judgment and for making us so readable on the page! This is Jeff's and my second book with Debby, and I'm delighted to work with both Jeff and Debby again. Our agent, Alexander Hoyt, provided wisdom and guidance in moving this project from idea to completion. Many thanks, Alex! Special thanks as well to my late friend and agent, Theron Raines, who helped me immensely before his untimely passing. In a project like this one, requiring charts and tables and a bunch of other statistical data, we were helped enormously by the contribution of my Lynx Investment Advisory colleague, Justin Ellsesser, CFA, CAIA. Justin, we couldn't have done it without you. Thanks as well to all my other colleagues at Lynx, including Safi and BRH for their support and friendship. Finally, special gratitude to Ann, for putting up with the hours I spent in somewhat solitary mode working on the book, and hoping she didn't enjoy them too much.

—*Peter Tanous*

This book comes together at a time when investors have experienced one of the most explosive bull markets in history. Despite the meteoric rise in stocks from the March 2009 lows, many investors remain on the sidelines, fearful that another crisis is just around the corner. Now, investors face another challenge, namely trying to navigate through an environment where market gains aren't going to be manufactured by central bank money printing.

While we're no wide-eyed optimists, Peter and I believe we have a formula to light the path ahead. With that in mind, I'd like to thank Peter again for his marvelous work and the inspiration to embark on our second journey through the world of finance and investing. This book came together due to brainpower from a variety of sources. I'd especially like to thank the brilliant Mohamed El-Erian at Allianz for his invaluable insights into the future; Liz Ann Sonders at Charles Schwab for her words of wisdom and unfailing patience with my incessant questions; and Jim Paulsen at Wells Capital Management, who is not only a skilled financial mind but also my comrade in the long-suffering legion known as Minnesota Vikings fanatics. Also thanks to Tom Lydon at ETFtrends.com who has been invaluable over the years in helping me understand the ever-evolving world of exchange-traded funds and donated his time specifically to the focus of this book.

I'm also proud to call Debby Englander our editor, again, and grateful to the expertise of our agent Alex Hoyt, who provided the impetus to get this work into the hands of the great people at Newsmax. A debt of gratitude also goes to the multiple folks along the way, too numerous to call out by name, who have provided encouragement and inspiration as we worked our way through the completion of this project. As a journalist, I'm humbled to have access to so many smart minds on Wall Street who are always willing to lend their expertise and, occasionally, to joust with me on live TV.

I'm doubly humbled to work at that storied institution known as CNBC, which is my home away from home, one of the finest news organizations on the planet and one that has been so wonderfully supportive for my various projects, including this one. Thanks to CNBC President Mark Hoffman as well as CNBC. com editors past and present including Jeff Nash, Ben Berkowitz, Christina Cheddar-Berk, Xana Antunes, and Allen Wastler.

Finally, of course, none of this happens, not one word of it, without the unfailing love, encouragement, and support of my wife, MaryEllen, who never lets me forget that there is no such thing as impossible.

—Jeff Cox

Why This Book Is Different

THE CONCEPT OF A "30-Minute Millionaire" may sound like a gimmick. But after you take a few minutes to understand the premise, you'll see that it's actually a viable strategy.

Start your timers.

Why Isn't Everybody a Millionaire?

There are lots of reasons, of course. But one of them shouldn't be that they don't have enough time. This goal is eminently attainable for many, many investors. We are not talking about the super-wealthy or individuals with mid-six-figure incomes. We're talking about people who are employed, have some savings, and who would love to figure out how to save and invest their money to build a lucrative nest egg. Does this sound like you?

Most investors fail not because they have too little information about investing, but because they are exposed to *too much* information about investing. Look around. Financial news is available from sources as near as our smartphones, not to mention newspapers, blogs, dedicated cable channels, and electronic alerts on just about anything that happens in the market economy. Is it any wonder that most investors emerge confused at the end of a typical day?

Why Isn't Everybody a Millionaire (Part 2)?

Some plan their retirement by stashing savings in banks, CDs, or Treasury bonds. These individuals are painfully aware of the lessons of the recent stock market crashes in 2000–2002 and 2007–2009. Others are willing to take some risk in the stock market by buying stocks they find attractive, or those that were recommended in the financial press or over the airwaves. But somehow these investors never seem to get ahead.

An Intelligent and Practical Strategy to Retire a Millionaire

We're going to show you how to become a millionaire by spending no more than 30 minutes a week on your investments and by adopting a relatively simple investment strategy that will see you through for years to come. This strategy relies on understanding what works in the markets, and understanding what doesn't.

And here's the key: successful investing is not really about how much time you spend doing it—it is about how smart you are with that time. We strongly believe that spending much more than 30 minutes a week is not only unnecessary but also counterproductive. Our job is to show you exactly what to look for and how to spend your time building and supervising the intelligent, well-balanced, risk-mitigated portfolio that will make you a millionaire.

What You Should Expect from Us

We are two individuals with a wealth of investment experience. Peter has nearly 50 years of experience in the investment field, and he is the author or co-author of six books on investments and the economy. Jeff is an acclaimed and award-winning financial journalist with CNBC and co-authored, with Peter, *Debt, Deficits, and the Demise of the American Economy* (Wiley, 2011). He appears almost daily on CNBC and has been a writer and editor for nearly 30 years.

We view our task not to *tell* you what to do, but rather to explain and convince you that this 30-minute strategy is the most sensible and intelligent approach to achieving your goal.

What We Need from You

We ask that you commit to saving an appropriate amount of money on a regular basis, weekly or monthly. These funds will be put aside and invested according to the plan we will give you. If you start early on, say, when you're in your twenties or thirties, you will need to save a lot less than if you start playing catch-up in your forties or fifties. Regardless of your current age, we'll show you the specific amounts you'll need to get to millionaire status, along with the strategies to get you there. The goals we will strive to achieve are not pie-in-the-sky objectives that assume a rate of growth that is practically and historically unrealistic. We know better, and you do, too. Many of the portfolio outcomes we will show you assume a rate of growth that is lower than the historic growth rate of the stock market.

You should approach this goal with a sense of discipline and habit, and we'll help you achieve that, too. No prior investment knowledge is needed, or even necessarily helpful. We'll keep everything simple, understandable, and even fun.

That's about it. Don't rush to read this book in one or two sittings. Let the material sink in slowly and securely. Soon you will be prepared to embark on your personal road to becoming a millionaire, once or several times over.

1

Investing:
What Works,
and What Doesn't

WHEN YOU'VE BEEN AROUND investing for several decades, you ought to have learned a few things. We believe we have. Consider your own experiences. How many people do you know who have bought a stock on rumors, or because someone famous on TV recommended it, or because a friend has a friend who is the nephew of the CEO of a company that is about to make a major medical breakthrough that will send the stock soaring? Yes, we've all been there. Most of us, however, don't keep falling for these traps forever. Losing money is painful, and making investments like these almost always result in a financial loss.

That's the first lesson. *Don't buy stocks on rumors or tips.* If your shoeshine boy or cabdriver thinks a company is hot stuff, chances are pretty good that you've already missed the boat. Hopefully, you already knew that.

Another common error is buying a mutual fund that has shown terrific performance over the last one or two years. Have you ever noticed that when you buy a fund like that, its performance mysteriously and suddenly goes into a steep downward spiral? Studies, including those conducted twice a year from the S&P Dow Jones Indices, have found consistently that past positive performance is frequently a measure of future poor performance. Most of us have made that mistake, too. But then the question becomes: if you can't pick a fund based on its track record, how will you make the right choice? That's a good query, and we'll explain it later in chapters 5 and 12.

One final example: You own a bunch of stocks or funds or both. The stock market turns ugly. *Your investments register a big paper loss. What do you do? In too many cases, you will sell out in a panic to protect whatever you have left.* That's what many investors did after the market meltdowns of 2000–2001 and 2008–2009.

These are just three examples of how not to make money in the stock market. There are others, but enough negativity for now. Let's get positive.

A few of the secrets to successful investing are, surprisingly, well known but not well followed. Most likely you've heard or read about the majority of them. This book is about what works, what doesn't, and, most importantly, how to spend a modest amount of time getting the strategies right and sticking with them.

So here are the basic rules. In the coming chapters we'll take you through some of the background of why the rules actually work. Once you understand why the rules are there, you'll find them easier to follow.

1. Successful Investing Works Best over the Long Term

Really? Yes, we've heard that for years. Big deal. But let's ground this rule in facts. The single best investment in American history has been the stock market. We have more than 100 years of records to prove it. As of 2015, stocks had produced an average

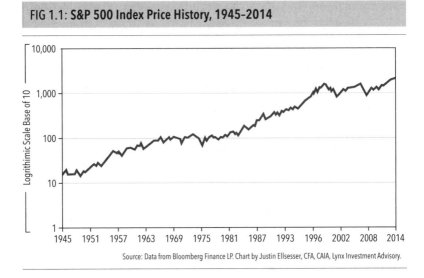

FIG 1.1: S&P 500 Index Price History, 1945-2014

Source: Data from Bloomberg Finance LP. Chart by Justin Ellsesser, CFA, CAIA, Lynx Investment Advisory.

annual return of over 10 percent (dividends included) for almost 70 years.

A chart of the S&P 500 going back almost 70 years appears in Figure 1.1.

Impressive, no? Based on the data, since 1945 stocks have returned an annualized 10.8 percent (including dividends). And if only those returns were in a nice straight line . . . but that isn't the way it works. (More on this phenomenon in coming chapters.)

Now let's divide the stock market returns into deciles, or periods of 10 years. Here is one example of a 10-year period in the stock market: from 1989 to 1999, stocks, as measured by the S&P 500, rose 19 percent a year for 10 years! Pretty impressive. If only . . .

But naturally, this is not typical.

Nor is this decade: from 1965 to 1974 the stock market declined, on average, 4.6 percent a year. Of course, the stock market didn't decline every year in that 10-year period, but an average annual loss of 4 percent would certainly discourage most investors.

These examples aren't the worst of the lot; they are just samples. And they reinforce the point that successful investing is a long-term game, for which you need to be prepared intellectually and psychologically. Getting rich is a function of patience, not how much time you spend learning the mechanics and theory of stock market investing.

To be a successful investor, you must base your actions and your faith in what has transpired through history.

2. Asset Allocation Is Really Important

Asset Allocation is the term used to explain portfolio diversification, and it's one we take for granted in the investment business. It refers to the different investments (assets), in stocks, bonds, and other items, that must be diversified intelligently by "allocating" *how much* of each of the different types of investments you want to own. It's important for a number of reasons.

First, do you really want all of your investments to move up and down at the same time? Probably not. Sure, if the market is going up, we're happy if *all* our investments are going up. It's the down markets that really concern us. When the market plunges, we need to own some investments that anchor our portfolio and reduce the volatility, and pain, while our stocks lose value. Back 20 or 30 years ago, a typical portfolio would be called "60/40," which meant that the portfolio was invested 60 percent in stocks and 40 percent in bonds. But this allocation was popular when bonds actually had decent yields of 5 percent, 6 percent, or even higher. Today most bonds yield next to nothing, so a contemporary 60/40 portfolio would mean that only 60 percent of the portfolio is invested and the rest is just, well, sitting there asleep, earning nothing.

The issue is that most portfolios aren't, and shouldn't be, invested 100 percent in the stock market. The stock market is generally the most volatile (read as "risky") asset class in which to invest. For most investors, a 100 percent allocation to stocks is just too risky. Stocks might go up substantially, but they can also drop dramatically in a short period of time. As a result, professional advisors recommend that you invest a portion of your portfolio in stocks, since stocks will provide the most growth, but also invest in securities that are less risky and perhaps offer a more certain, if smaller, return. These are the decisions that comprise the asset allocation process. We'll get into more details in chapter 5. It's really important that you understand the concept of asset allocation to help you make the decisions appropriate to your investment goals.

The good news about this process is that it need not be done very often. If you get it right early on, there's generally little need to change it. Of course, there will be occasions to tweak the allocation. For example, if stocks rise too far and reach euphoric levels, we never know when the euphoria's going to end, but we know that it will. At times like these, it may be advisable to reduce the amount of your portfolio invested in stocks (the riskiest asset class) and increase the allocation to safer investments, such as funds invested in bonds or preferred stocks.

Spending too much time on the asset allocation process will inevitably be counterproductive, since changes in the allocation should be done rarely. This is another good example of why 30 minutes a week is all you need to manage an effective portfolio.

3. Don't Buy Stocks!

What? You just said that stocks were the best performing assets in the US, but now you're telling me not to buy them?

Not exactly. What we mean is that you should let the professionals buy stocks for you. Don't pick them on your own. This is another example of how many investors waste time in a failed attempt to achieve good investment performance. Yes, that sounds harsh, but look at it this way: suppose you are one of the millions of investors who picks stocks on their own. For starters, since it's your money, you'll likely do some research on the stocks that interest you. That means Internet searches, research reports, and perhaps conversations with brokers or research analysts. This process takes time. Then again, you have a day job, don't you? How much time do you really have to devote to this activity? If you're serious and motivated, you might spend an hour each day researching companies and stocks you're interested in buying. And that's a big investment of your time.

Now think about all those professional money managers and fund managers who trained for a career in researching and purchasing stocks. How much time do they spend on this activity? Well, if this is their sole job, we can assume that they spend upwards of eight hours a day, can't we? Now answer this question: if you're spending an hour or so a day researching stocks, how are you going to do a better job than a professional who spends up to eight hours a day doing the same thing? That's a tough question, but the answer should be obvious: the professional fund manager is likely to make more informed, better researched choices than you are. And if you somehow beat the market consistently, you may call yourself very talented. Meaning no disrespect, we might call you very lucky.

Our advice is not to pick stocks; instead pick mutual funds, ETFs, or index funds. This will take far less time and the odds are in your favor. Besides, monitoring these investments will be a snap, and we'll discuss why in more detail. Spending less time on your investments will likely be more productive and rewarding.

4. Own (Some) Commodities!
We mentioned earlier that the traditional portfolio of the past was a "60/40" allocation—60 percent to stocks and 40 percent to bonds.

Today's smart portfolios include more than just US stocks and bonds. In keeping with the objective to reduce risk through effective asset allocation, well-diversified portfolios also have allocations to emerging market equities and bonds, European equities, master limited partnerships, exchange-traded funds (ETFs), and several commodities, the most important being gold. Commodities refer to the physical assets that investors trade in, ranging from the proverbial pork bellies, wheat, corn, and other farm products, to precious metals like silver, platinum, and gold. Gold is bought through an ETF, such as GLD and others, or an investor can elect to purchase gold mining stocks.

No matter how you buy it, gold is a very volatile commodity, so it must be sized in a portfolio with that volatility in mind. In other words, the allocation will be relatively small. We will discuss why we believe investors should own gold in chapter 7.

5. Bonds Again?

While 60 percent of your portfolio should still be invested in stocks, bonds have yielded so little in recent times that your bond allocation might as well have been sitting in cash, earning nothing. Over the past few years, bonds have actually performed well, since bond prices go up as interest rates come down. You see, as interest rates decline, newer bonds offer a lower interest rate than the older ones did, so the older bonds with the higher interest rate are worth more than the newer ones with the lower interest rate. Still, in recent times, the yield has been so low as to offer little in the way of return on your investment.

That may now have changed. In December 2015, The Federal Reserve raised interest rates by 0.25 percent, the first increase in interest rates since June 2006. This is a big deal since, if interest rates continue to rise, bonds will once again become attractive for their yield, provided, and this is important, that you buy short-term bonds. Remember the example of bond prices going up as interest rates went down? The reverse is also true. If interest rates continue to rise, the bonds with the lower interest rates are worth less than the newer bonds with a higher interest rate. To be sure you are getting the higher interest rate, you want your existing bonds to mature quickly so they can be replaced with bonds earning higher interest in a rising interest rate environment.

Don't be concerned about picking bonds. Here again, we'll recommend funds with professional managers to do the picking for you. And the funds we'll recommend will have mostly short to intermediate term maturities so you won't get locked into a long-term bond should interest rates continue to rise.

6. Understand Risk

Fear is the most pervasive cause of stock market losses. When markets go down, many investors panic and pull out their investments. This attempt to stop further losses, and salvage their assets after the decline, is a mistake. What we are really talking about here are emotions—not usually the subject of investment books.

Say hello to a new area of economics: behavioral economics. Interest in this branch of the dismal science, which deals with our human, emotional, and psychological reactions to investing, has been rising. Indeed, the world took notice of behavioral economics when, in 2002, economist Daniel Kahneman won the Nobel Prize in economics. His work on how emotions affect decision-making in investing shed a new light on the human factors involved in effective and rewarding investing.

While we can't predict human behavior, or even change it much, our contention is that if you, as an investor, have a deeper understanding of risk, you will be better prepared to handle it. Understanding risk is likely to make it easier for you to deal with market losses. It's all part of the game. There is no reward without risk. For that reason, we've included a special chapter, chapter 12, that is all about risk.

These are the basics, intended to provide a good starting point on the investment strategies discussed throughout the rest of the book. Everything we do from here on will be designed to prepare you for the portfolio you will use for a lifetime. We'll show you how to spend your 30 minutes a week on the monitoring and changes that matter, while not wasting your time on investment practices that have proven useless.

2

Can You Really Get Rich Buying Stocks?

BY LOOKING AT THE long-term record of stock market gains, you already know that you can get rich buying stocks. If there's been a problem, it's been a lack of patience. You must stay invested over the long term. That may sound easy, but history has shown that it's not. Many investors panic and jump out of the stock market at precisely the wrong time. This is largely a function of irrational investment decisions based on emotion. The emotional factors that influence these decisions have spawned a new and popular field of economic study.

The stock market has yielded an average return of around 9 percent a year since the end of World War II. But when we look at various time periods, we see a pattern of erratic returns that can last for years. In the previous chapter, we showed examples of two 10-year periods, one with terrific returns and one with inferior returns.

Let's look at some additional periods to hammer this point home.

To start, we'll divide the stock market returns into deciles again. Here are some examples of 10-year periods in the stock market with both good returns and poor returns.

Let's start with an example of a terrific decade in stocks: from January 1, 1991 to December 31, 2000, stocks, as measured by the S&P 500, rose 18.0 percent a year (on average) for a decade! Now look at the decade after this one, from January 1, 2001 to December 31, 2010. During that period, the stock market rose only 1.1 percent a year for 10 years, a very disappointing performance. During this period, you would have been better off leaving your money in a commercial bank savings account, which would have provided a higher return with no risk.

You get the point. Sadly, none of us can predict which decade, or even which year, will be good or bad for stocks. Yes, we know there are many prognosticators and market prophets out there attempting to predict the market on a daily, weekly, monthly, or annual basis. But so far, none has succeeded, except by luck, and none over a long period of time. So if your retirement, or your kid's college education, is a number of years into the future, your best odds of financial success, proven throughout history, is to invest in the stock market. And to succeed, you must train yourself to stick with it.

Predicting the future is impossible, so none of your 30 minutes a week will be spent figuring out where the market is going next. As we continue, you'll see our 30-Minute Millionaire idea come into focus. It's not a gimmick. It works because we eliminate all of the activities that contribute nothing to your investment success. High on that list is trying to figure out where the stock market is going. You won't waste time consulting crystal balls, stargazing, or any similar activities that serve no useful purpose. This will free up time to spend on the investment activities that will definitely help you succeed.

Forgive us in advance, but we're going to harp on factors that we know lead to success. That means we'll occasionally sound repetitive.

There's a reason we do this: by repeating the essentials, we will remind you of the habitual practices you need to lock into your memory.

In the end, by spending time only on those investment activities that work, and by ignoring those that don't, we can tell you with confidence that 30 minutes a week is all you will need to be successful. (Does this sound repetitive?)

Why Does Long-Term Investing Work?

This is an important question. Imagine if you asked, "What if these gains in stock market prices just stop?" The reason stocks go up is simply because the United States economy is growing. As gross domestic product (GDP)—the measure of our economic health—grows, so will the fortunes of successful companies. In our competitive environment, we know that not every company will succeed. But with population growth due to the rise of family formations and increased prosperity, the economy will also continue to grow. We take this growth, which has persisted over the long term since the country was founded, as a given.

As the economy grows, the stock market—a proxy for the economy—also grows.

Why Aren't More Stock Market Investors Rich?

The answer to that reasonable question is precisely the point of this book: most investors *spend too much time*, not too little, on their investments. The extra time they spend is generally to get an edge on the market, to outsmart other investors, or to uncover those hidden gems all the experts talk about. And, that is simply a waste of time.

The story below is but one example of many others of its kind. In this case, this is the tale of a janitor who died in 2014, as reported in February of 2015 by CNBC:

> Ronald Read, a Vermont gas station attendant and janitor, invested in recognizable names when he amassed an $8 million fortune, according to his attorney. A large part of that

fortune was later bequeathed to an area library and hospital after his death, stunning a community that had no idea
about his wealth.

Most of Read's investments were found in a safe deposit box,
Read's attorney, Laurie Rowell, told CNBC. Those investments included AT&T, Bank of America, CVS, Deere, GE
and General Motors.

"He only invested in what he knew and what paid dividends.
That was important to him," she said in an interview with
"Closing Bell."

Read, who died at 92, has been described as quiet and frugal.
No one appeared to have any idea that he was so wealthy,
including his stepchildren, Rowell said.[1]

Read was a gas station attendant and a janitor, not a stock market expert with an MBA, but he amassed a fortune greater than
the wealth of the vast majority of investors. How was this possible? Did Mr. Read pore over *The Wall Street Journal* every day?
Did he comb through research reports from the top investment
firms? Did he study and follow market trends and charts?
No.
He bought what he knew, and he was a patient investor. He
bought stocks in companies he recognized and that grew with
the economy. Above all, he had patience and lived with his investments for decades, until he died at age 92.
The preceding example raises the question: if you're a long-
term investor, why not just put all of your money in a stock market mutual fund and wait to get rich? Ah, if only it were so simple!
Theoretically, that actually might work. But various factors—
importantly, the human one—suggest that it just won't work for
you. Your animal instincts may thwart the success of this simple
plan. Major market swoons scare most investors into getting out
of the market or lightening up.

As we have seen, there are many examples of entire decades of poor market performance—a fact that will discourage all but the hardiest investors. That's why most investment professionals, including us, recommend a diversified portfolio invested not only in stocks, but also in other asset classes whose performance does not mirror that of the stock market. Our challenge is to help you get the asset allocation right, while spending a reasonable amount of time tweaking your portfolio once it has been created successfully.

We hope we're getting the point across: investing success is not a function of how much time you put into it. It is a function of how smart you are with the time you spend. Thirty minutes a week is about the right amount you'll need to be a successful and smart investor.

3

Why Doesn't Everyone Get Rich in the Stock Market?

WE CAN HEAR YOU asking, "If stocks held for the long term create wealth, why aren't more people rich?"

Indeed. It seems so simple: buy stocks in well-known companies, sit back, do nothing, and get rich. Janitors have done it. People with no expertise at all have done it. But how come many smart people have *not* done it?

We've already covered the basic fault: a lack of patience. You've probably heard about people who lived in semi-poverty but left millions of dollars behind when they died. These stories are ones of neglect—not neglect of the individual, but neglect of his or her portfolio! These people invested consistently and methodically over time, through thick and thin. They didn't read investment books or *The Wall Street Journal*, or listen to financial news on their radio or TV. They just continued to invest.

The reality is that few people will exercise the discipline, or have the luck, of the fortunate ones who make millions of dollars in the stock market without really trying. You need a different plan, one that will work for the vast majority of individuals who truly want to get rich but have neither the time, nor energy, nor discipline to spend hours upon hours following the stock market and studying all the information that encompasses the investment process.

Peter Lynch was the manager of the Fidelity Magellan fund; under his leadership it achieved an unbelievable performance record of 29 percent per year over 13 years, from 1977 to 1990. Just $10,000 invested in his fund in 1977 grew to $280,000 13 years later. Then he quit. Peter Lynch was, and is, an investment legend, the possessor of a performance record that will arguably never be beat.

So how did he do it?

You want to know? No problem. He'll tell you. In fact, he wrote not one, but three popular investment books in which he told readers *exactly* how he piled up the best performance record in mutual fund history. Secret formulas? A magic selection process? Hidden clues? Nope. In fact, you'll be shocked at some of the ways this guru picked stocks.

Lynch told stories of how he'd take his wife and kids to the mall to see what would happen. He would give his kids some money, his wife had her own, and see how they would spend it. The kids invariably went to The Gap and bought clothes. Peter Lynch noticed that there were many other kids in the store browsing and shopping. Bingo! He bought the stock.

He also told the story of how he came to buy stock in Hanes. At the time, the company was test marketing a new product in Boston called L'Eggs. His wife bought a pair, loved them, and raved to Peter about them. Guess what? Peter bought the stock, and it did very well.

If you're like most of us, you're not going to find this advice very useful. You might be thinking, "Oh yeah, go to the mall, watch what people are buying, buy the stock, and retire rich. Sure."

Yet Peter Lynch did just that. Then he went on to write books telling people how he picked the stocks that would go up, in some cases, by multiples of 10 (he called them "ten-baggers").

After my book *Investment Gurus* came out, I (Peter) went on the talk circuit. The book featured Peter Lynch, so the phenomenon of his success would invariably come up. I'd ask the group, "How many of you have read one of Peter Lynch's books?" A lot of hands would go up. Then I'd ask how many of them had made fortunes after reading Peter Lynch's books. No hands would go up.

The fact of the matter is that Lynch is a phenomenon of nature, a brilliant investor whose brain is wired differently from ours. His skill as a stock picker can't be taught. Think about other brilliant investors such as Warren Buffett and George Soros. We can't emulate their success either, no matter how willing they might be to share their "secrets" with us.

If you believe what we're saying, this may be the last investment book you need. The process is accessible and easy to follow, and it takes just 30 minutes a week.

The secret to your investment success is learning where and how to spend your precious time on your investment plan. We've talked about some of the common and popular methods that don't work: Don't pick stocks; let the professionals do that. Diversify your investments intelligently; we'll show you how. Add some commodities to your investment portfolio; we'll explain. Ignore stock tips and rumors; but you already knew that.

An Essential Ingredient: Discipline

We mentioned early on that we are asking for your focus and discipline. For many of us, discipline means adhering to instructions or rules. Being in the Army comes to mind. Children know what discipline means, too: do what you're told or suffer the consequences. As adults, most discipline needs to be self-imposed, and that is what we're advocating. You need to stick to the plan, even if interruptions cause you to deviate temporarily. To make the task easier, most of the effort necessary will be front-loaded—though the title of the book suggests you'll only need to spend 30 minutes a week to achieve success, you'll need to spend more than that up front. And, obviously, it will take you more than 30 minutes to read this book! As you read on, we'll get into the nuts and bolts of building your portfolio and how to monitor and tweak it as necessary.

We're making progress.

4

30 Minutes? Seriously

PART OF THE KEY to learning how to manage your future is unlearning the mistakes of your past. This is not always easy. As humans, we develop habits that feel comfortable, and they're hard to relinquish. The greatest obstacle is pride. Once we've done something often enough, we convince ourselves that we have mastered the art, and we don't need to learn anything else. We are frail of ego, though many of us would hesitate to admit it, and changing a learned behavioral pattern seems anathema to us.

Ever have someone try to give you some friendly advice on the golf course that you refuse to take? How about that gentle cajoling from your spouse that maybe you should have gotten off at the last exit? Even taking advice from your boss can be tough, particularly when you're frightened that admitting a blunder could make you look weak, and perhaps jeopardize your future with the company.

Your future as a good investor will require a change in mindset, particularly from what you've been conditioned to believe in the years since the financial crisis.

The bad news is that the days of easy money are over. That doesn't mean there isn't money to be made, there's plenty in fact, but it's going to require more skill than simply throwing money at the market and watching it grow. One of the main reasons for the boom years from mid-2009 through the writing of this book was that the market was underpinned with liquidity. Trillions of dollars had been floating through the financial markets thanks to the largess from the Federal Reserve and its counterparts around the world. The US central bank, which sets interest rates and decides monetary policy, began flooding the markets with money after the collapse of the banking system nearly capsized the global economy. It made life easy for investors.

With bond yields driven to historic lows, the real estate market in the tank, and commodity prices falling in the face of a global slowdown, there really was no place aside from stocks to put your money. As a result, stock markets, particularly in the US, surged dramatically. The Fed kept monetary policy loose and looked to push money toward risk assets, equities in particular. The S&P 500 gained more than 200 percent from the crisis low of March 2009 over the next six years—one of the biggest bull markets in history.

Good for you if you were lucky enough to take part in the stock surge. You were in the minority. Many folks, who otherwise would have been invested, took a powder after the financial crisis and never came back. As 2015 dawned, money market funds, which yield basically zero, still held some $2.7 trillion in cash. Think about that number: that's more than $8,500 for every man, woman, and child in the United States, lying fallow in an account, drawing almost no interest, and missing out on a rocket-fueled market. What a pity, considering all the millionaires that could have been made out there with just a little savvy and a modest appetite for risk.

The truth is that becoming a millionaire is easy. Don't believe us? Here's the math: say you're 25 years old. You've just gotten married, and between you and your spouse, you make the median household income of $53,046. Together you contribute 6 percent of your salary to a 401(k) plan. Your bosses match that contribution up to 4 percent. Through the course of your working career, you average a 3 percent salary increase per year. For the purpose of this example, your annual rate of return is just 5 percent.

These are all extremely conservative estimates. Many of you who are conscious investors may have an income above the median level. A 6 percent contribution is ambitious if you're living paycheck-to-paycheck, but if you've freed yourself from that burden, you won't even miss the contribution after a few pay periods. The 5 percent market return is considerably below the historical average, which was 9.4 percent annualized even through the dark days of the financial crisis and recovery from 2005 to 2014.

So what happens when we put all these assumptions together? You get a balance of $1,028,964 in your account when you retire at age 65. Congratulations, you are a millionaire! And just think what happens if you start playing with a few of these numbers. Imagine if you're able to become a "10 and 10" investor, putting away 10 percent of your income, considered the ideal by many advisors, and earning an optimistic, but not unrealistic, return of 10 percent. Using the same assumptions as in the earlier example, your retirement balance would be $4,358,159. You just went from a comfortable lifestyle to one of a snowbird with a winter condo in Florida near a golf course, where you can spend your golden years trying to break 80.

Sounds easy, doesn't it? So why aren't there more gray-haired millionaires strolling the fairways of the local country club? Why do we still watch the incessant TV commercials pitching reverse mortgages and cut-rate life insurance to folks who shouldn't have a financial care in the world? Why doesn't every hardworking man and woman with access either to a 401(k) or an IRA have a burgeoning nest egg? Why do people continue to have worries about retirement?

It's because something happens on the road from a wide-eyed youth to a weary senior: life.

Life is what happens to you while you're putting away 5 to 10 percent of your income year after year, hoping to retire a millionaire (or so John Lennon might have said if he was an investment advisor). Life is a ho-hum job after college that barely pays enough for you to handle your student debt. Life is a wife and family, a new home with a big down payment, a car, your kids' doctor bills, a leaky roof, and a new water heater. Then, out of nowhere, a crisis reverberates through the entire global economy, sacks Wall Street, and tears a vicious hole through your financial planning. Due to a bunch of soulless, greedy goons, your 401(k) has now been turned into a 201(k) or a 101(k), and all your marvelous plans have been ruined.

Yes, life.

Life is hard, but investing is supposed to be easy. Now, forget for a moment all those high-flying guys you see in the movies, such as the Gordon Gekkos, the "Wolves," and everyone else in the wildly romanticized tales of the whacky and wild Wall Street life. While there are obviously various shreds of truth in those sordid tales that Hollywood brings us with such gusto, investing—that is, saving for the future, developing investment goals, and following through in a carefully orchestrated manner—should be easy. And don't tell Oliver Stone we said this, but investing should also be kind of boring. The road to real riches is not lined with Lamborghinis and paved with Cartier gold, but rather is best traveled at the speed limit or even a bit below, obeying the signs along the way and focusing on getting to the destination with as few bumps and bruises as possible.

Can you find your way to your goals by just dedicating 30 minutes a week? Of course you can.

A few years ago, Bankrate.com—a reputable and resourceful guide for investors, market watchers, and home buyers—asked its readers what they would do if they could turn time back to their twenties when the whole world was like an ocean before the first big wave hit.[1] The responses were telling. Rather than elaborate thoughts about manipulating specific moments that shaped their lives, most of what ordinary folks said was simple: they would have thought a little further ahead, disciplined themselves a bit more, and maybe used 30 minutes a week to make better financial decisions. A few sample responses:

> I would have saved 10 percent automatically from my paycheck by direct deposit into a savings account earning the best possible interest compounded daily. I would have also disciplined myself to deposit 10 percent of any additional money from gifts, refunds or other earned income.

> I would have bought a small house outright with the money I had saved (instead of renting an apartment for over 30 years).

> I would have found a job that I loved and devoted my life to it. At least you could be happy even if you were not where you wanted to be financially.

> Hope this helps someone out there.

Also:

> I regret not starting an IRA when in my 20s. If I could do it over again, I would have 10 percent of my income automatically taken out of my pay and have it invested. The interest is enticing but the compounding of interest over one's working years would make for a very, very comfortable retirement. Hakuna matata!

And this:

I'm 50 years old. I've made some awful financial mistakes. What I would tell young people is, learn to read markets. Learn to read the stock market. Learn to read the real estate markets. Learn to read any market you're interested in. I still have time, but it's going to be a nail-biter, especially in today's markets. If I had only known how to read 20 years ago.[2]

Look carefully. Put aside what you can afford. Take the time to understand what's happening around you. Get some basic knowledge. Learn to seek advice, but only take that advice if it makes sense and meshes with your plans for the future.

One of the recurring themes you'll see in this book is our strong belief that there is such a thing as being too informed, particularly when it comes to investing. More specifically, you can be too tuned in to the news cycle. Now you may find that a curious thing to say considering one of us (Jeff) makes a living bringing the headlines home to readers of CNBC.com and viewers of CNBC on a daily basis.

A typical news day for business reporters on Wall Street starts before sunrise, and it goes something like this: first, they eyeball what happened in the overnight markets. Is Asia up or down? What kind of day is Europe having so far? Then they look at the US futures, which gives an indication of what kind of a day fast-moving traders are expecting in the markets. All the players in the financial markets then gather around their TV screens at 8:30 a.m. for the day's key economic report (there aren't data releases every day, but most days). The New York Stock Exchange then opens at 9:30, and away we go. There's company news, political developments, speeches from Federal Reserve officials, and analyst notes hitting the tape—a potpourri of highly-intriguing and relevant information in its own right, but only pertinent to the 30-Minute Millionaire when absorbed with the right perspective in mind.

What do we mean when we talk about "perspective"? We mean you should be a news watcher but not a news chaser. While the endless gush of news that comes through the ether should inform your decisions, you shouldn't be making long-term investment decisions based on short-term gyrations. While it's all well and good to dissect the monthly nonfarm payrolls report when it hits the first Friday of each month, even such an important economic data point needs to be considered in perspective.

Your focus shouldn't be on one month's data but rather three, six, and twelve months of information from the Bureau of Labor Statistics, which releases voluminous data each month on the state of the American jobs market. Ditto for all the other information you are barraged with on a minute-by-minute basis. It's all well and good for you to have a grasp on what's happening on a macro level, but your investment decisions should focus on the long term. Informed investors generally make smarter decisions, but you want to avoid information overload. (Later in this book we'll have more on where you can get the most important data you'll need for long-term investment decisions.)

Now we know that despite our admonitions, you may still be tempted to get caught up in the whirlwind pace of day-to-day and minute-to-minute news. We ask that you again consider the example of Ronald Read, the 92-year-old janitor from Vermont who died in early 2015 and left behind a staggering $8 million fortune. No part of that last sentence was a misprint. This unassuming man who drove a used Toyota quietly amassed a huge sum of money, made all the more stunning because nobody around him—not friends, family, or neighbors—knew he had built up that much. The only remote clue anyone had was that he liked to read *The Wall Street Journal*.

Read's lawyer, Laurie Rowell, told CNBC that Read made his mountain of money with a blue-chip portfolio that included meat-and-potatoes companies like AT&T, Bank of America, CVS, Deere, and General Motor. It's fair to say he didn't chase the latest flavor-of-the-week in the stock market. Suffice to say this is not the sexiest portfolio in the world. AT&T was a company that vastly underperformed the market during its rally off the March 2009 financial crisis lows. Bank of America lumbered through the crisis with the ill-advised acquisition of subprime lender Countrywide Financial and some other questionable moves. CVS, however, quadrupled in price during the recovery, while Deere more than tripled during that period and has been a top market performer for more than a decade. As for GM, well, we're not in the habit of recommending companies that need periodic defibrillation from the government to survive, but at least the company pays a nice dividend.

They key takeaway is that Mr. Read put aside what had to be modest sums of money from his jobs as a gas station attendant and janitor at J.C. Penney and stuck with what he knew. We'll go out on a limb here and guess that Ronald, outside of reading *The Wall Street Journal*, rarely put in more than 30 minutes a week on his personal road to riches.

"You'd never know the man was a millionaire," Rowell said. "The last time he came here, he parked far away in a spot where there were no meters so he could save the coins."[3] Upon his death, Mr. Read bequeathed $1.2 million to the Brooks Memorial Library and $4.8 million to the Brattleboro Memorial Hospital.

Now they know.

5

The Power of Passive

VEN LEON COOPERMAN HAS a bad year every now and then. The humble hedge fund superstar, known as much for his uncanny ability to pick winners as for his unassuming personal style, steered his usually unflappable ship into the rocks in 2014.

When the rest of the market was having a solid, if not stunning, year with a 13.5 percent return on the S&P 500, Cooperman and his $13 billion Omega Advisors firm found the sailing much rougher. Thanks in large part to some wrong-way bets on energy stocks, during a year in which oil prices plummeted and sent the industry into a tailspin, Cooperman actually lost 2.13 percent for the year.[1] It was quite a turn of events for a manager who once, at CNBC's annual "Delivering Alpha" conference, nailed 10 out of 10 stock picks to have positive returns over the following year. In 2014, though, he saw his portfolio get stuck with losers like SandRidge Energy, Atlas Energy, and QEP Resources. All three companies seemed like reasonable enough investments at the start of the year, but they failed to deliver. For once, the great Leon Cooperman, or "Lee" as he is more commonly known, had to face some negative headlines.

Of course, as time marches on, Cooperman's clients likely will forget one bad year, and deservedly so. He's had an extraordinary run of success, delivering annualized returns of 14 percent, net of fees, since 1991.[2] It's believed that 2014 was the first time his fund took a loss when the S&P 500 showed a gain. With a track record like that, he's likely to bounce back. And it's certainly not our intention to pick on Lee, who not only is a terrific investor but, by all accounts, a decent person as well. So, if you've got an extra couple of million lying around that you don't mind tying up in a hedge fund for a few years, and you have a strong appetite for risk, by all means try your luck and see if the highly selective Omega will take you on as a client.

But stock-picking is a terribly difficult game. Few people are any good at it, and even then their records are usually spotty at best. A groundbreaking study of active management by S&P Dow Jones Indices found that more than 86 percent of active fund managers failed to deliver better returns than their basic benchmarks in 2014. The results were no better tracking back three, five, and ten years, with 76.5 percent of all active managers underperforming

TABLE 5.1: Performance of Benchmarks

Category	Index	1 year	3 years	5 years	10 years
All US equity	S&P Comp 500	87.23%	76.77%	80.82%	76.54%
All large-cap	S&P 500	86.44%	76.25%	88.65%	82.07%
All mid-cap	S&P MidCap 500	66.23%	70.48%	85.37%	89.71%
All small-cap	S&P Small Cap 600	72.92%	80.40%	86.55%	87.75%

Source: Aye M. Soe, "SPIVA US Scorecard," March 2015 (Index Research and Design, S&P Dow Jones Indices, 2015).

during the prior ten years. Table 5.1 lists some broad categories of stock types, the indexes they track, and the percent of active managers who fell short of those indexes over the past several time periods.

This is why we sincerely encourage you to leave the stock picking to the pros. There are better, easier ways for you to make money in the market. And, yes, you can do it in 30 minutes a week.

"Passive" investing sounds really boring. The name conjures visions of someone who throws money in a couple different places and then sits back and hopes for strong, consistent returns. Nothing could be further from the truth. Passive investing still requires acumen. It demands informed decision-making and, at times, requires an iron gut willing to take a level of calculated risk to try to maximize profits or take advantage of opportunities. What it does not entail, however, is active stock picking, continuous trades in and out of positions, and the terribly misguided willingness of trying to time markets.

There are a couple fairly basic concepts at the core of passive investing with which you should be acquainted. The first is the index. A key element toward becoming a 30-Minute Millionaire is to know the names, and understand the functions, of the main indexes used by market experts. The most basic ones are those you hear about virtually every day, with the most ubiquitous being the one commonly referred to as "the Dow." Though it's become virtually synonymous with stock market performance, the truth behind this index is a little more complicated.

"The Dow" is actually the Dow Jones Industrial Average, an index made up of 30 stocks designed to represent the basic components of the American economy. There's Caterpillar, which represents construction; Energy giants ExxonMobil and Chevron; Johnson & Johnson and Procter & Gamble as proxies for the consumer; JPMorgan Chase and Goldman Sachs for banking; and McDonald's, which gives a picture of discretionary food spending. Oh, and now there's Apple of course, which represents pretty much the future of, well, everything. There are 21 other companies that stand in for various other components of our economy.

Traders on Wall Street, however, don't focus as much on the Dow as TV pundits or casual market watchers. Instead, they look to the S&P 500 as a broader gauge. As implied by the name, the index consists of 500 companies that cover an even wider swath than the Dow. The S&P 500 is divided into 10 major sectors: consumer discretionary, consumer staples, financials, energy, utilities, healthcare, industrials, materials, information technology, and telecommunications. There are a myriad of other subsectors.

The third of the three "major indexes," as they are sometimes referred to, is the Nasdaq. You've probably often heard financial commentators refer to this index with the stock line, "the tech-heavy Nasdaq." There's good reason for that, as this index is relatively new to the game and consists primarily of technology-related companies like Apple, Facebook, and Intel. There are some non-tech companies in there, too, such as Starbucks and Costco, but they are few and far between. The Nasdaq reading we hear discussed during the day's market activity is the Nasdaq Composite, which, as of early 2015, consisted of more than 4,800 companies.

These indexes, however, are just three of hundreds out there tracking stocks, bonds, and commodities in categories that span the entire gamut of investing. They can entail macro concepts, like the three we've discussed here, or drill down much further into the financial markets and their various asset classes. There are indexes that cover each sector in the S&P 500; ones that span any number of other sub-indices in the Dow; those that measure commodities; bond indexes that track government and corporate debt; and many, many more. There are even a whole slew of indexes that do nothing else but measure market volatility across all of the aforementioned groupings.

Why have all these indexes? Well, they serve a number of purposes. For economists, they provide an easy picture on how various aspects of the economy are performing. If, for instance, economists want to gauge the health of the consumer, they can drill down through measures that look at the performance of the consumer staples sector through its own index. If they want to dig a little deeper, there are measures that look at home furnishings, household appliances, and footwear. Many of these sub-industries have their very own indexes that measure the underlying companies within their industries, and their stock performance.

Now that's all well and good if you're an economist, but what if you're an investor who only has 30 minutes a week to dedicate to portfolio management? Indexes, most importantly of all, provide investment opportunities. There are multiple funds out there that do nothing else than track these indexes by investing in the same companies that comprise them. We're going to do a much deeper dive into this subject later in the book when we talk about exchange-traded funds (ETFs), but let's take a quick look at what kind of opportunities index investing provides.

Say, for instance, that at the outset of 2014, you and your professional investment advisor have found that the US and global economy are on their collective way up, and you want to get in on the action. One of the areas that you think will benefit from this growth is the industrial sector. All of that expansion is going to need infrastructure, and you want to be investing in some of the companies that provide highways, power, equipment, and the like, that will get the economic wheels rolling.

There are two ways to implement this investing strategy: you either can pick a few companies that you think are going to hit it big, or you can invest in a fund that provides broad-based exposure to the sector, minimizing the legwork and your exposure to risk. State Street has a popular exchange-traded fund called the SPDR Industrial Select Sector. Its ticker is XLI, and this fund has a number of blue-chip companies in its portfolio, including General Electric, Union Pacific, and 3M (a few of its biggest holdings at the start of 2015).

GE is a fine company, one of the most durable in US history, but its 2014 performance was ugly, losing about 9.5 percent. Both Union Pacific and 3M, however, outperformed the market, with Union Pacific going up a gaudy 42 percent and 3M increasing by 19 percent. The performance of other companies in the industrial sector varied widely. For example, United Technologies, the fourth-largest holding by XLI, rose only modestly for the year. But if you bought XLI, you were protected from intra-sector fluctuations because the fund had a mix of companies that kept you afloat in an otherwise so-so year for the industrial sector.

Yes, we know what you're going to say: "Gosh, we could have just picked Union Pacific, had a great year, and not been weighed down by the rest of the sector." Good luck with that strategy. GE is one of the most-owned stocks on the market, and its performance over the years has been, to say the least, spotty. That means a whole lot of people who invested in this industrial bulwark got it wrong. Don't believe us that stock picking is tough? GameStop was the most-shorted stock on the S&P 500 at the beginning of 2015—more than 44 percent of its shares outstanding were being shorted, or bet against—and all the company did was gain 14.4 percent in the first two months of the year. Plucking a stock out of the thousands of companies out there is tough business.

Still skeptical about the virtues of index investing? During one of Warren Buffett's periodic appearances on CNBC, NBA's Cleveland Cavaliers basketball player LeBron James asked, via remote video, how he should invest his fortune. Did one of the greatest investors in history let King James in on the latest big thing? Did he pass along some hotshot new stock he was looking into? You'd think Buffett at least would have tried to steer James and his $270 million fortune into a few shares of Berkshire Hathaway, right? No, the Oracle of Omaha's words could not have been more precise, prescient, or, you might say, pedestrian:

"Actually, for the rest of his career and beyond, in terms of earnings power then, just making monthly investments in a low-cost index fund makes a lot of sense," Buffett advised.[3] "Somebody in his position ought to have a significant cash reserve, whatever makes him comfortable, and then beyond that owning a piece of America, a diversified piece over time, held for 30 or 40 years, is bound to do well. The income will go up over the years and there's really nothing to worry about."

Clean. Clear. Simple. There's no need to go hunting for the next big thing when the ability to invest in high performance at comparatively low cost is near at hand. Of course, if that was all there was to investing we could close the book right here and send you on your merry way. There is plenty more to it, and if you really want to live the life of the 30-Minute Millionaire, you're going to need to do more than merely sit back and watch some plain-vanilla fund pull in high-single-digit returns year after year.

The world is changing. One of the cornerstones of this book's thesis is that we're entering an era of lower returns that will last for a considerable period of time. In the six years following the financial crisis lows in early March 2009, the S&P 500 gained more than 200 percent. History tells us that sustaining that kind of pace is, if not impossible, extremely unlikely. That doesn't mean the market can't keep going up—indeed, it's a historical certainty that at some point down the road the market will be higher than it is on the day you're reading this—but the pace of gains will slow. There will be bear markets, market corrections, and episodes of extreme volatility. No matter how the ball bounces, you can be assured that investors face a more uncertain environment ahead.

Most bull markets last about four years. (The post-Great Recession run was going six years and counting as of this book's writing.) Only four bull markets have ever made it to their sixth year, and the most recent one had the biggest gain of any run that long. Why does this matter? Because of a concept called "mean reversion."

The "mean" is another word for the "average," which we arrive at by adding up all the numbers in a series and then dividing the resulting number by the amount of items in that series. In terms of investing, mean reversion implies that eventually, almost always, everything will revert to the mean, or its typical return, over time. A very simple analysis of mean reversion, as it relates to the post-crisis market, is that after many years of above-average returns, multiple years of below-average returns will be needed to bring things back into sync. But there's more to this than simple historical trends.

Robert Shiller is a brilliant economist, a Nobel Prize winner who was one of the few who foresaw the real estate crash, and subsequent banking collapse, that caused the Great Recession. He also is the creator of the Cyclically Adjusted Price-Earnings Ratio, or CAPE. The CAPE looks at stock market values in a way different than the many analysts who focus only on near-term earnings, whether they be trailing (in the past) or forward (future) earnings. Shiller's CAPE uses a 10-year history of earnings, smoothing out some of the periodic distortions and fluctuations that happen in corporate cycles and coming up with a number that determines proper market value.

The CAPE is not a perfect measure—no market barometer is—but it has helped provide a pretty good roadmap over time about the valuation of the stock market. By the time 2015 rolled around, the market had a CAPE value in excess of 24, compared to a historic level around 18. By the time you are reading this, that level could be a little higher or a little lower. Either way, there's little doubt that market valuation has become stretched during the post-crisis rebound. A reckoning is in store.

So where does that leave you? Well, it takes us to the final concept we'll explore in this chapter about the power of passive: rebalancing. You're likely familiar with the 60/40 mix that many recommend for the mix of your portfolio. That's the ballpark figure for allocation of 60 percent stocks, commodities, and other risk assets to 40 percent fixed income and cash. In fact, it has become so ubiquitous an investing maxim because it makes a lot of sense. Your portfolio should be weighted toward riskier assets like stocks, but it should also include a counterweight of bonds and cash for safe-haven purposes in times of turmoil. There will, however, be times when you'll want more than 60 percent allocated toward stocks and, of course, more than 40 percent toward bonds. In the world of the 30-Minute Millionaire, how diversification is achieved is about to change in a meaningful way. The old 60/40 may not serve you so well in the days ahead. The main thing you have to keep in mind for now is that it will take work and know-how to keep a portfolio properly balanced. Optimum asset allocation doesn't happen alone.

What happens, for instance, if stocks have a great year that overshadows the gain in bonds? Over the three years from 2012 to 2014, the S&P 500 had annualized gains of 18 percent. During the same period, the Barclays US Aggregate Bond Index, which is a broad measure of fixed income performance, had annualized gains of 2.4 percent. You can imagine what that might do to portfolio allocation. You could have gone into 2012 with a perfect 60/40 balance in your portfolio, but after three years of such aggressive returns for stocks, and such substandard returns for bonds, you would now have a much stronger weighting toward equities than fixed income. This is a problem.

If you've ever looked at any kind of investor materials—be it a company prospectus, an analyst note, or an economic analysis—you no doubt have come across some variation of this familiar disclaimer: "Past performance is no guarantee of future results." Know this sentence, commit it to memory, and repeat it to yourself periodically so you never forget that when it comes to investing, past is not always prologue. Just because one part of your portfolio showed spectacular returns this year does not mean a repeat is in store next year. The same applies to companies: today's next big thing, like the dotcom boom that happened in the late 1990s, is tomorrow's Pets.com, which became a poster child for high-flying Internet companies that crashed and burned when the boom went bust.

In addition to knowing what's in your portfolio, you also need to know how much of each asset is there. Put another way, if you've started out the year with a perfect risk-to-safety allocation in your portfolio, and stocks and commodities have had a big year while bonds and cash have lost out, chances are good your portfolio is out of balance. While the temptation to go with the hot hand is sometimes irresistible, at some point in time the level of risk you're taking is going to keep you up at night.

So at this point you want to start selling a few of your winners to build up a little dry powder for those rainy days that can be the worst enemy of those caught flat-footed or the best friend to those who can smell an opportunity. Remember "buy low and sell high"? That tried and true market strategy is best executed by investors who aren't afraid to take a profit. Taking that profit and getting your asset allocation back in sync with your risk tolerance is what rebalancing, and sound investing, is really all about.

One large investment house, in a presentation to clients about the differences, as well as the advantages and disadvantages, of active and passive management, described the latter in these terms:

> [P]assive strategies are simpler. There are no decisions on the part of the investor beyond selecting the index. All acquisition and disposition decisions are made automatically based on index constituent changes. For those investors who lack the time necessary to research active managers or individual investments, a passive strategy may be an appropriate alternative.[4]

While there is truth in this statement, at least in the conventional sense of passive management, the investor of the future, the 30-Minute Millionaire, is not going to employ this type of passive strategy. Rather, the passive investor is going to be a decision-maker and, at times, a risk-taker—someone who understands that the right strategy is going to be more important than the right stocks. In the next several chapters we're going to go into even more detail about how this is going to happen. Indeed, what we're about to describe is going to change everything.

6

Understanding ETFs

JACK BOGLE IS, QUITE simply, one of the most brilliant investors who has ever lived. So when he talks, you should listen. In 1974, Jack founded The Vanguard Group, an investment management company that grew into a $3 trillion testament to sound investing practices—a place where investors could get practical advice, particularly in times of market turmoil. Jack Bogle told investors to keep their heads during the 2008 financial crisis, counseling them not to cave, even when it looked like the market was losing its collective mind. And it's been Bogle, even in his mid-eighties and in semi-retirement, who has continued to warn investors against chasing returns, trying to time markets, and, of course, venturing to pick stocks.

Bogle's investing theses are, in a very broad sense, in line with the philosophy that we counsel for the 30-Minute Millionaire. He believes in using low-cost funds that track basic market

indexes—a practice that, of course, jibes quite well with what we
have discussed thus far. The way Bogle sees it, active investors out
running around picking stocks, even if they are good at it, will
not achieve the same returns as index investors, due to the simple
cost inherent in buying and selling individual stocks. These costs
include advisory fees, marketing, technology costs associated
with trading platforms, and a whole slew of other items.

"When we look at the big picture of the costs of investing,
including sales loads as well as expense ratios and cash drag, it
is a foregone conclusion that active investors, in aggregate, will
underperform index investors. It's the mathematics," Bogle said
in a 2014 interview with Charles Rotblut of the American Association of Individual Investors.[1]

Bogle is also an ardent opponent of exchange-traded funds,
or ETFs. ETFs look and sound a lot like the Vanguard 500 Index
mutual fund that Bogle created, to great Wall Street ridicule, in
1976. Nobody thought people would bite on a product that was
tied only to a basic market index and didn't promise the outsized
returns that active managers pitched (and to which they so often
failed to deliver). The difference between an ETF and one of the
many mutual funds that Bogle helped develop at Vanguard is
that the former acts more like a stock in the way investors can
access it. ETFs can be traded during regular market hours, unlike
a mutual fund, which can only change hands after trading is over.

While Bogle's Vanguard funds carry some of the lowest expense
ratios in the industry, ETFs, as a whole, are still far cheaper than
mutual funds. They carry only modest expenses and have tax
advantages as well. Simply put, an ETF looks and sounds like a
mutual fund but it trades like a stock, without all of the inherent
risk of individual equities.

Bogle's distaste for ETFs essentially stems from a belief that
they've morphed into a bastardization of what he created all those
years ago. More specifically, he objects to people using ETFs as
stocks, buying and selling sector bets the way a day trader would

buy and sell any stock that appears to display some sort of pricing irregularity. He's particularly critical of those who dabble in some of the more exotic instruments in the industry. For instance, there are funds that promise double and triple the returns of their respective indexes. Others are "short" funds, meaning they pay off if an index falls in value, some of which also use leverage to deliver double and triple the moves of their underlying index.

You can see the problem pretty easily here: all is well and good if the market is trending your way. Investors in one triple-levered fund that bet against crude oil, which crashed in June 2014, saw gains of more than 400 percent. Those who had a fund from the same outfit with the same leverage, but that was predicated on rising oil, lost 93 percent during the same period. The problem is that virtually no one saw the crash in oil prices coming. The ones who did and bet triple on it got lucky. The vast majority of investors who thought the oil bull market would continue, lost almost everything. Bogle called people who invest in these exotic instruments "fruitcakes, nut cases, and lunatic fringe."[2] We're inclined to agree—this is no way to become a 30-Minute Millionaire.

We start this chapter about ETFs with Jack Bogle's critique because we think it's important to know the risks before you can appreciate the rewards. Bogle is right that these funds should not be traded willy-nilly. But there is too much to like about ETFs to not make them a significant part of your 30-Minute Millionaire strategy.

After all, despite his criticism, Bogle's Vanguard, from which he retired as CEO in the late 1990s, has become a major player in the industry. In fact, Vanguard is one of three companies that control more than three-fourths of the entire ETF market in the US. It is sandwiched between BlackRock and SSgA (State Street), with the three firms boasting some $1.7 trillion of the total $2.1 trillion in assets as of the spring of 2015.[3]

The first ETF came to market in 1993, when State Street launched the SPDR S&P 500, a plain-vanilla fund that tracked the index of the same name and has come to be known in market circles as the "Spider." In the years that followed, there would be Spider funds created for each of the 10 sectors in the S&P 500, as well as for multiple other sectors and strategies that spanned the market.

For most of their early existence, ETFs were considered the purview of traders. The funds could be used to execute various approaches to investing, particularly including portfolio hedging. Traders kept the sector funds in their portfolios as a way to brace against whipsaw changes in the market. As the industry blossomed, and the amount of funds created swelled towards 1,700, the products became more ubiquitous and available to retail investors, who now make up about half the ownership of ETFs. In fact, in the 12-month period from the end of the first quarter in 2014 to the end of the first quarter in 2015, more retail (mom-and-pop) investor money went into ETFs than mutual funds—the first time that has ever happened.

In 2014, speaking at Bloomberg's annual investor conference in New York, Bogle recalled that when he heard about the idea for the Spider, he thought creating a way to actively trade a passive index-following strategy was the dumbest idea he'd ever heard.[4] But whether Bogle likes it or not, the truth is that ETFs are going to play a major role in the way both traders and mom-and-pop investors interact with financial markets in the future.

In addition to the advantages already cited—ease of trade, low costs, and tax advantages—ETFs are providing investors with ever-evolving ways to execute perfectly rational strategies. For instance, currency hedging, protecting against the ups and downs of money in various countries, is going to be a pivotal part of investing.

The world's central banks, such as the European Central Bank and the Bank of Japan, are in an aggressive cycle of devaluing their currencies that is going to last for years. At the same time, the US Federal Reserve probably will be taking actions that will strengthen the dollar. Hedging against those movements previously involved some heavy strategy and complicated moves. Now, however, investors simply can buy one of the many growing hedging products on the market to protect their investments.

Each January, ETF.com holds a conference in Hollywood, Florida, called "Inside ETFs." (Co-author Jeff Cox covers the event for CNBC.) Over the years, the evolution of this conference has been stunning. Where it was once a low-profile gathering of investors seriously involved in what was long considered a niche industry, the 2015 version was staggeringly different.

Big-name bond investor Jeff Gundlach of DoubleLine Capital was one of the principal speakers. High-profile political operatives James Carville and Karl Rove duked it out on stage. A crowd of hundreds had swelled to thousands, and the nights were filled with swanky yacht parties, private dinners for deep-pocketed investors, and a general air that ETFs had, well, grown up. One of the most striking trends was the proliferation of fund managers peddling all sorts of exotic products, from "smart-beta" funds that were invested in far-flung locales around the world, to what may well be the most important development in the industry: actively managed funds.

Yes, we just spent an entire chapter expounding on the virtues of passive investing, and we indeed believe that a large part of the 30-Minute Millionaire's portfolio will be passive in nature. Just as we believe, however, that every portfolio should have some exposure to gold and precious metals, we also believe that there should be exposure to active strategies as well. By active, we mean an allocation toward strategies that hone in on certain areas of the market that can provide lucrative returns. Your portfolios, however, will be properly balanced with passive investments that make sure risks remain limited.

The active part of the ETF industry is surging in popularity. In 2014, the number of actively managed exchange-traded funds swelled from a net of 73 to 125. There were 55 new funds introduced, which was more than the previous three years combined.

Managed assets for these funds expanded by $2.4 billion to $17.265 billion, representing a 16.5 percent gain.

Thus far, the greatest interest in the active space is in fixed income funds. This is understandable considering that clipping coupons on bonds doesn't make a lot of sense these days, since they have such low yields. Active managers trade bonds in hopes of price appreciation that results from demand. Consequently, the big players in the active ETF field are firms like Pimco—the Newport Beach, California-based bond giant that had $1.7 trillion in total assets under management in 2015. Pimco led all players in the actively managed ETF space with $6.8 billion under management in that specific realm. Other leaders include First Trust and WisdomTree.

As for the types of active funds, about half the total assets were concentrated in either short-term or global bonds. US equity funds made up just 3.8 percent of the total. The popularity of active ETFs, however, is likely only in its early stages. A more equal distribution of funds will come as the sector matures and investors begin to better understand how active funds work.

One interesting area of growth in the actively managed space is so-called tactical funds. These types of funds employ active strategies using ETFs, rather than individual stocks, to execute. In some ways, this may sound appealing. After all, we agree that the old rules don't apply. The days of the 60/40 stocks-to-bonds split aren't going to continue in the world we see ahead. It's a world where volatility will reign on a global stage and where central banks will battle it out to see who can be more effective at printing money, devaluing currency, and trying to push investors into risk. It will be a world in which geopolitical conflicts will matter more than ever; where a tectonic shift in energy will change the way the global economy keeps its growth engine running; and where technology will reshape the means of communication in ways that we haven't yet even begun to ponder.

Tactical funds fit into this world because they're capable, at least in theory, of rebalancing on the run. The idea is to have a fund that can pivot between sector allocations and a change in focus on particular countries or various other strategies. Tactical funds can help investors mitigate risks over the short term by building defensive strategies against changing conditions. It's probably no wonder that tactical funds were 2014's biggest gainer in terms of assets under management. The 15 active tactical ETFs on the market managed $1.2 billion in investor cash and represented more than 7 percent of the total market share in the active ETF space.

Despite investor interest, it's hard to fully evaluate tactical ETFs at this point. Many of the newcomers only have a few million dollars in assets and, since they're lightly traded, they are subject to high levels of volatility. They also are focused on short-term moves, something we don't advocate much for 30-Minute Millionaires.

As things stand, there are 15 different kinds of actively managed ETFs: short-term bond, global bond, alternative income, alternative, tactical, foreign bond, high-yield, US equity, currency, US bond, multi-asset, foreign equity, global equity, alternative bond, and sustainable. Why so many? The investment world is changing, and exchange-traded funds will be one of the areas at the forefront of what's happening.

And, yes, the 30-Minute Millionaire is going to have to make some portfolio room for active management.

7

You Still Need Gold

CIVILIZED BARROOMS THROUGHOUT THE ages traditionally have con- sidered two topics off limits: politics and religion. Both issues inspire strong enough emotions that taking too emphatic a posi- tion can get you an express ticket to a black eye or worse.

You might want to add gold to that list of subjects where you should dare not go, particularly in saloons where the talk may turn to investing. Few topics these days can get people as riled up as the yellow metal and how it should fit into investment portfolios. On one side are the gold bugs: they believe in gold with a near-reli- gious fervor. Those at the most extreme edges see gold as an indis- pensable safety valve against the looming monetary apocalypse. They believe that once the world's central bankers completely destroy the value of fiat currencies, the only refuge will be gold.

On the other side are the apostles who worship at the church of Keynesianism. It was John Maynard Keynes, of course, who is

remembered for calling gold a "barbarous relic" because it basically had outlived its usefulness. (His remarks actually were more
specifically directed at the gold standard rather than gold itself,
but the quote still stands.) Charlie Munger, Warren Buffett's
right-hand man at Berkshire Hathaway, put a bit less delicate
touch on it when he made this proclamation to anyone owning
gold: "You're a jerk."[1]

"Civilized people don't own gold," Munger added during a
CNBC interview in which he said gold's last useful stint was for
Jewish families to sew inside their clothes as they escaped the
Holocaust.[2] You probably don't want to be in a barroom with
Charlie Munger. With this kind of fiery talk, trouble could ensue.

Where, though, does the truth lie when it comes to gold?

As "civilized" investors should know by now, reality sits somewhere in the middle of cuckoo late-night infomercial conspira-
cies and the utter dismissiveness by sophisticated investors who
should know better. Gold, we believe, remains an integral part
of any investor's diversified portfolio. Sure, it might not appeal
to those who can buy ketchup companies and railroads like
they're pieces on a Monopoly board. But for those with an interest in hedging against unpredictable events, who believe there's a
need for non-correlated assets, and who see a greater likelihood
of inflation rather than deflation ahead, gold is a tremendously
effective choice.

We've talked about the impact the Federal Reserve and its
unstoppable printing press has had on financial markets and your
investments. Every time stocks have headed south since the 2008
financial crisis, the Fed has stepped in to create money out of thin
air and levitate asset prices. Three rounds of quantitative easing
accompanied gains on the S&P 500 of more than 200 percent.
The Fed's low interest-rate policy has kept bond yields artificially
low, allowing corporate America to spend trillions on stock buybacks and dividend issuance—a tremendous misallocation of
resources that has caused massive distortions in all areas of the

capital markets. And while the Fed is gradually dialing down its cheap-money policies, central banks across the globe are just getting started. While no other efforts similar to the Fed's are likely to have as substantial an impact, investors will be left to wrestle with the ramifications of ultra-easy global monetary policy for at least the next generation.

There have been less visible effects of monetary policy that the 30-Minute Millionaire needs to know as well. All that easing has tamped down volatility, the normal movement of asset classes up and down and in different directions from each other. Like inflation, and chocolate, volatility is healthy in reasonable doses. A certain level of volatility in the market provides opportunities for long-term investors to capitalize on undervalued and overvalued sectors. It allows short-term traders to exploit weaknesses in pricing, and, in turn, makes the overall market healthier by evening out disparities. Volatility signals that markets are healthy, that the ups and downs that are part of the business cycle and the normal routine of investors are alive and well.

Excessive Fed intervention, however, pretty much crushed stock market volatility since quantitative easing began in 2008. Though there have been periodic spikes, equity investors have been able to rest assured that whenever things got a little out of hand on Wall Street, the Fed would to step in with its monetary balm. The most common measure of market volatility, imprecise though it may be, is the aptly named Volatility Index, a gauge the Chicago Board Options Exchange (CBOE) derives by comparing calls (the option to buy a stock) against puts (the option to sell). What the CBOE ends up with is the "Vix," also sometimes called the "Fear Index."

During the worst of the 2008 financial crisis, the Vix zoomed all the way to 80 in those harrowing days around the time when Lehman Brothers collapsed. Over the course of the next couple of years, there would be peaks and valleys, but once the Fed kicked off QE3 in 2011, with its promise of unlimited and eternal easing, that was pretty much the end of the road for the Vix, and for market volatility. Except for a brief jolt in October 2014, the Vix would never see the north side of 30 again. This was a stunning 75 percent tumble from the crisis days and a reflection of how boring the market had become.

With the precipitous volatility decline came a rise in correlation, which describes the rise and fall of asset classes in unison. You might have heard television experts refer to "risk-on" and "risk-off" days in the market. That's a neat way of describing a high-correlation environment. "Risk-on" means it's time to buy everything. "Risk-off" means it's time to sell everything.

There were comparatively few in-betweens. Either traders were buying, or they were selling. The post-crisis period has seen almost perfect correlations in various stock market sectors, as well as in individual stocks, certain commodities, currencies, and bond yields. Why does this matter? Because rising correlations make a diversified portfolio nearly impossible. The logic isn't hard to fathom: at its core, diversification requires differentiation so you want some investments that zig when others zag. This is especially important when things are heading south. We want assets in our portfolios that will rise when others, particularly stocks, are falling. Over time, there has been one investment that has outperformed all others in providing differentiation.

We speak, of course, of gold. Before, during, and after the crisis, gold has been the best thing to own as an insurance policy against stock market declines. Indeed, it is the ultimate non-correlated asset. From 1970 until 2013, gold had a correlation of −.0057 to the S&P 500. To explain, correlations are calculated on a scale of −1 to +1. Large-cap stocks, as you would expect, have a correlation score of 1.0, indicating that they are perfectly in sync with the S&P 500, which is a large-cap index. During that time period, a balanced stocks and bonds portfolio had a score of 0.9392, indicating a strong correlation of about 94 percent of the time, while long-term government bonds scored a 0.0883, or less than 9 percent correlation with the direction of the S&P 500—pretty good, but not as good as gold, to borrow a phrase.

This discussion about gold as a non-correlated asset might seem a bit granular, but it's important because it amplifies the need for gold allocation in our portfolios beyond some of the more obvious reasons. The inflation and fiat currency arguments are highly important, indeed almost low-hanging fruit at this point. If you've contemplated gold as an investment, you'll be at least vaguely familiar with both points. But the importance of having an asset that will protect you during bad times is perhaps the least sexy, though most important, reason why you need to invest in gold. Now, let's look at some of the others.

Inflation, in one form or another, is a regular part of American life. We all know it costs more to live now than it did five, ten, or twenty years ago. Yet for much of the post-financial crisis period we were fed a steady diet of misinformation and obfuscation from egghead government statisticians that inflation was "muted" and that the spikes we saw in various costs of living were, in the favorite terminology of former Fed Chairman Ben Bernanke and his acolytes, "transitory." Monthly releases of data points like the Consumer Price Index, or the Personal Consumption Expenditures reading, the Fed's preferred measure, showed inflation hovering between 1 and 2 percent. Those of us on the ground, though, knew differently.

In April 1995, the typical price for a gallon of unleaded gasoline was $1.16. In April 2015, that would have translated into an inflation-adjusted price of $1.83, given that during the period inflation rose in aggregate about 55 percent, as calculated by the Bureau of Labor Statistics. The actual price in April 2015, though, was closer to $2.65 a gallon, a 128 percent increase, and that was even after the major tumble prices saw from June 2014 to March 2015. In April 1995, a pound of ground beef cost you $1.84. In April 2015, you were paying $4.32, a 134 percent increase. If ground beef had merely kept up with the inflation rate reported by the government, that price should have been only $2.86.

We could go on and on, but you get the point: inflation, as a measure of price increases in the lives of ordinary Americans, has been rising rapidly, far more than simple government measures would indicate, while the Fed has been playing Wall Street's Santa Claus. So how does gold fit in to this equation?

Here's a very simple measure: in our 1995 reference point, gold was trading around $400 an ounce. If it had tracked the same inflation multiple we used in our gasoline and ground beef computation, gold should have been about $621 an ounce in 2015. Instead, it was hovering around $1,200, or nearly double the rate of inflation. In simple price terms, gold's tripling easily outdistanced the soaring inflation rates of gasoline and ground beef.

Gold also has an admirable performance record against the stock market. Over a 10-year time period from early 2004 to early 2014, a gold-only portfolio would have generated annualized returns of 12.8 percent versus an S&P 500-only portfolio with 7.2 percent. More than that, gold didn't have the stomach-churning volatility the stock market experienced when Bear Stearns and Lehman Brothers were no more and Wall Street descended into chaos. The last ones left standing were gold investors, in a scenario bound to be repeated in the years ahead, as global central banks try to reflate struggling economies and money printing goes viral.

Gold, in fact, would have enjoyed an even better rally had the central banks done their job a little better. Try as they did, the Fed, the Bank of Japan, the European Central Bank, and multiple other counterparts were only able to do so much to pump their economies back to life. Despite all of the Fed's efforts, the US had yet to achieve annualized growth above 2.5 percent through 2014. Japanese Prime Minister Shinzo Abe similarly gave his country a bit of a boost, but inflation remained in check. The ECB's Mario Draghi struggled to keep his jurisdiction out of recession, but profligate debt prevented the Eurozone from achieving escape velocity.

So while the Fed appears on course to begin a very gradual tightening of monetary policy as the unemployment rate keeps moving lower, don't expect the same course for its brethren. The monetary taps will remain open for years. Even though the yellow metal overshot in 2011—reaching $1,908 an ounce before tumbling lower on realizations that the willingness of central banks to deal with today's troubles tomorrow was virtually unlimited—long-term investors shouldn't be upset. In fact, the decline set up a splendid re-entry point. The fundamental case for gold remains.

The prospects ahead for central bank activity present something of a win-win scenario for gold investors. At some point, the trillions in liquidity floating around will generate that long-sought inflation, likely at crisis levels. For instance, at some point Greece is going to have to quit the euro zone and reinstitute its own currency (the drachma) so it can inflate its way out of debt. Money velocity is on the increase in the US as well, with M1 and M2 measures, which look at the flow of money through the system, rising respectively at 7.3 percent and 5.8 percent levels from May 2014 through May 2015, even as the Fed was unshackling itself from QE. Concurrently, gold will continue to exhibit its safe-haven characteristics, serving as the asset of choice for many investors in times of financial market turmoil.

Let's look at a few more explanations of why central bank activity will provide even more reasons to own gold. They have been substantial buyers of this commodity in recent years, and that buying is likely to accelerate. The broad trend has been well in place since the financial crisis rattled investor confidence in the global economy and monetary authorities have sought buffers against further disruptions. Central bank gold buying jumped from 2 percent of total global demand in 2010 to 14 percent in 2014, a stunning rise during a period of flux for gold prices.

Here's the take on central bank activity, according to the World Gold Council, a London-based advisory group:

This change in behavior is a clear acknowledgment of the benefits that gold can bring to a reserve portfolio. Some banks have bought gold to diversify their portfolios, especially from US$-denominated assets, with which gold has a strong negative correlation. Others have bought gold as a hedge against tail risks or because of its inflation-hedging characteristics (gold has a long history of maintaining its purchasing power).

Gold plays a prominent role in reserve asset management, as it is one of the few assets that is universally permitted by the investment guidelines of the world's central banks. This is in part due to the gold market being deep and liquid, which is a key characteristic required by reserve asset managers.[3]

Central bank net gold purchases increased 17 consecutive quarters through the first three months of 2015, indicating if not a sign of extreme price appreciation then definitely a floor. As Bloomberg pointed out, the total purchases would have been enough to buy 75 Boeing Dreamliners, each of which costs in the neighborhood of $300 million. Global governments added 477.2 metric tons of gold to their reserves, in contrast to a two-decade trend of selling that began in the late 1980s, which equated to the second-biggest total ever. The biggest buyer was Russia.

"We expect official purchases to be one of several factors that boost gold prices in the next year or two, despite the prospect of tighter US monetary policy and renewed strength in the US dollar against other major currencies," Capital Economics, a top global forecasting firm, said in a report for clients on gold's prospects.

So should you find yourself in a saloon late at night, when the spirits have been flowing freely, and the talk turns to gold, keep a few things in mind should you decide to enter the fray. The future for gold should be prosperous. Monetary meddling among the Fed, ECB, BoJ, and any number of others in the central bank fraternity will drive substantial demand for gold. How substantial?

Well, we'd caution you before you line up on the gold bugs' side of the bar. While we think there's a much stronger case for inflation ahead, the threat of deflation driven by plodding global economic growth cannot be ignored. It's enough for us to caution you against believing that gold should be the cornerstone of your portfolio—it shouldn't. But a 5 percent allocation provides excellent protection against a number of storm clouds ahead and gives you a nice non-correlated asset to go one way when everything else is going the other. You can take that to the bank, and to the corner bar.

8

Buffett Rules

THERE'S A REASON WHY we didn't call this book "The 30-Minute Billionaire." Aside from lacking the same alliterative punch as *The 30-Minute Millionaire*, the assertion that you could become a billionaire by only dedicating a few minutes each week to your portfolio would be utter nonsense. Billionaires have followed all their own paths on the road to extreme riches, all of which are difficult to copy.

Of those 1,826 fortunate souls to make their way onto *Forbes'* billionaires list in 2015, 1,191 fell into the "self-made" classification, while 230 were simply born billionaires. The remaining folks were born with a considerable head start but then used their acumen on various levels to increase their wealth. After all, it indeed usually takes at least some money to make money, and nowhere is that truer than on the extreme periphery of the wealth scale.

But just because their lives seem so removed from ours doesn't mean there isn't plenty to learn from the ultra-rich. Very few of us are going to emulate, say, Mark Zuckerberg and come up with a seemingly trivial idea, like developing an online meeting place for college friends, that turns into a billion dollar business. If you look in the right places, though, and break things down far enough, you'll find plenty of useful nuggets for your path to becoming a 30-Minute Millionaire, even if you don't completely follow the Facebook founder's road to success.

Nowhere is this more apparent than with Warren Buffett, the Oracle of Omaha, who built a business empire at Berkshire Hathaway by following a remarkably simple set of rules: understand the companies in which you invest, don't chase returns, and don't expect to make a lot of money by taking on a lot of debt. Also, learn how to take a loss, don't invest for the short term, and believe in America and the things that make it great. Sound reasonable? It should, because virtually every move Buffett has ever made is in line with these very simple and practical principles.

While we're fans of some of Buffett's rules that we're about to explain, there are several areas where we'll at least slightly diverge. For one, we think you should try to be *like* Buffett without actually trying to *be* Buffett. After all, he's made his fortune picking individual stocks and making them part of a portfolio filled with companies that provide bread-and-butter services like insurance, rails, and consumer staple food products. Picking stocks takes a lot of time, research, and insight that most of us don't have to dedicate as we live our daily lives.

Even the pros who do pick stocks are generally not very good at it. In 2014 alone, fewer than 1 in 5 managers of active funds, stock pickers at their core, outperformed simple benchmark indexes like the S&P 500. Fortunately, we believe the 30-Minute Millionaire of the future won't need to pick stocks. Rather, we see a world where the profitable retail investors will leave the work to others, like Buffett.

His $72 billion fortune started with a few shares of a company called Cities Service and a vow—we're not making this up—to jump off the tallest building in Omaha if he hadn't made his first million by the time he turned 30. Obviously, Buffett never had to make that leap. Instead, he used the remarkable strides he made in business to guarantee that his first million was only the first of many, many more to come. This remarkable story of a self-made billionaire came about because Buffett followed a number of basic investing maxims, quoted ad nauseam through the years but always worth repeating:

- "Price is what you pay. Value is what you get."

- "After all, you only find out who is swimming naked when the tide goes out."

- "It takes 20 years to build a reputation and five minutes to ruin it."

- "The most important thing to do if you find yourself in a hole is to stop digging."

- "The asset I most value, aside from health, is interesting, diverse, and long-standing friends."[1]

These are all wonderful truisms. They reflect invaluable lessons, not only about investing but also life. But of all the quotes in the world according to Warren that we love, this one is the most important: "Be fearful when others are greedy, and be greedy when others are fearful."[2]

The wisdom of this quote is self-evident: at its core, investing is a game of emotions, with the two most prevalent and important being fear and greed. Watch the financial markets long enough and you'll learn that fear is at its peak when the market is falling the hardest, while greed reaches its apex when the market is soaring.

Nothing particularly illuminating there, of course—it's terrifying to watch your portfolio diminish and invigorating to watch it grow. Here's the thing, though: the wise investor, the 30-Minute Millionaire, knows this is the exact opposite of how your investing approach should work. A roaring bull market should raise red flags, or at least a yellow warning light, in any good investor's eyes. A plunging bear market should trigger a whole different set of signals. Are the falling market values justified? Has the selling been overdone? Are there bargains out there you should be on the lookout for? In short, as greed amps up, you should start worrying, and as fear spreads, start making out your shopping list for investments that are going to be had at bargain-basement prices.

Now, this does not mean that you should be selling reflexively into a bull market. But there are going to be times when you'll want to trim your sails. As the great, old market maxim goes: "Nobody ever went broke taking a profit." When you hear talking heads on TV speaking about getting yourself some "dry powder," they mean raising cash. You raise cash by selling some of your positions at various intervals, then adding when you find a better entry point. Conversely, this doesn't necessarily mean you should be on a buying frenzy during a bear market. There are going to be times when the market sells off for completely justifiable reasons. Every steep bear market in history, however, has presented investors with a significant buying opportunity at one point or another. The financial crisis slide, in which the major market averages lost about 60 percent, was no exception.

Let's go back to our Warren Buffett quote about being fearful when others are greedy, and greedy when others are fearful. Buffett made this comment in an op-ed piece he penned for the *New York Times* on October 16, 2008. We'll take a moment to revisit the scene: Bear Stearns, a Wall Street institution for generations, had collapsed the previous March and, at the US government's behest, had been absorbed by JPMorgan Chase. Six months later, the Bear Stearns situation turned out not to be the bottom of the financial crisis but merely a shot across the bow.

Lehman Brothers, an even more significant institution in the world of Wall Street, lost the confidence of its banking brethren and no longer could secure the short-term financing on which it relied for its existence. A historic weekend of wrangling—led by Treasury Secretary Henry Paulson, Federal Reserve Chairman Ben Bernanke, and New York Fed President Timothy Geithner— failed to find anyone willing to bail Lehman out. The following Monday, the bank had to file for bankruptcy, setting off a cataclysmic series of events that saw the world's financing mechanisms go into lockdown. Fear spread that other major institutions, like American International Group (AIG) and Merrill Lynch, were next. Bank lending shut down. The stock market crashed. Greed was gone, and fear was rampant.

In the middle of this financial apocalypse comes Warren Buffett, essentially waving his arms up and down, telling America to keep calm and carry on. His *Times* piece carried a headline at the time that seemed bombastic and naïve: "Buy American. I am." And no, Buffett wasn't talking about Levi's jeans, Budweiser beer, or a Ford truck. He was talking about American *stocks*.

What was the American market doing at the time? The S&P 500 had declined about 40 percent after reaching its historic peak almost a year to the day when Buffett's overture to America appeared. Amid a decidedly unfavorable time for American equities, Buffett felt strongly about the market, and his logic was hard to dispute. His words serve as a good lesson for all the aspiring 30-Minute Millionaires out there:

> Let me be clear on one point: I can't predict the short-term movements of the stock market. I haven't the faintest idea as to whether stocks will be higher or lower a month—or a year—from now. What is likely, however, is that the market will move higher, perhaps substantially so, well before either sentiment or the economy turns up. So if you wait for the robins, spring will be over.[3]

Yet the market's losses were far from over. The S&P 500 would tumble another 30 percent before finally making a bottom in March 2009. That bottoming point would be highly significant though, as it set the stage for one of the strongest bull markets in history. Buffett wanted investors to know that the markets had been here before, and, generally speaking, bad times presented big opportunities. More specifically, he pointed to three periods in history that were good buying times for investors—many of whom nonetheless sold every time the headlines turned difficult: 1932, during the Great Depression, when the market hit a low but rallied even as economic conditions deteriorated; 1942, when US fortunes in World War II had not yet turned in the Allies' favor; and the early 1980s, when the economy was in the death grip of inflation. Buffett rued the way investors reacted to individual news events rather than held tight to investing principles:

> Over the long term, the stock market news will be good. In the 20th century, the United States endured two world wars and other traumatic and expensive military conflicts; the Depression; a dozen or so recessions and financial panics; oil shocks; a flu epidemic; and the resignation of a disgraced president. Yet the Dow rose from 66 to 11,497.

> You might think it would have been impossible for an investor to lose money during a century marked by such an extraordinary gain. But some investors did. The hapless ones bought stocks only when they felt comfort in doing so and then proceeded to sell when the headlines made them queasy.[4]

Now, reducing something as complicated as the global financial markets, and the US market in particular, to folksy bromides is a risky business. Remember then, if you will, some other pretty solid advice, most often attributed to the economist John Maynard Keynes: "The market can remain irrational longer than you can remain solvent." So we know there are always risks, substantial at times, to investing. But, most often, the greater risk has been to not be invested.

We go back then, to our earlier point about wanting to be like Buffett without actually trying to be him (especially as it pertains to some of his limousine liberal political views). The idea of solvency is important. One of the reasons Buffett can stand in place during a rough patch for the market and the economy is that, as someone with a net worth of $72 billion, he can well afford the luxury of not panicking. But how do you, the retail investor, get into the same place?

This is about mindset as much as money. The reason Buffett doesn't panic in times of crises is that he has enough confidence in his portfolio to withstand an ill wind. He buys for the long term and only sells when he feels a company's value has deteriorated and offers too little for the future—not because everyone else is bailing. The panic versus fear quote we cited earlier on enters heavily into this philosophy. Times of panic bring opportunity; times of greed breed danger. Act accordingly.

Yet there's an even bigger idea here that fits more directly into our belief that you can be a 30-Minute Millionaire. As we've said, spending too much time thinking about your investments not only can be less productive but actually *counterproductive* to your financial well-being. (Yes, you can spend too much time on your portfolio.) Shockingly enough, there also is such a thing as too much information.

Information surrounds us, and nowhere is that more relevant than in the financial markets. There is now a round-the-clock surfeit of information for investors. We can track the movement of foreign markets in real time. Traders can react in milliseconds to data on Chinese export prices, Greek bond yields, or American mergers and acquisitions. High-speed computers are trained to recognize certain key words that come through the transom, sent out either through conventional means, like news wires, or the hottest new vehicle for market insiders: Twitter. Yes, a social media network in which users communicate information to each other in 140-character messages has become an integral part of the Wall Street network.

If it all seems a bit too much sometimes, well, it is. The 30-Minute Millionaire knows that while all of this back-and-forth transmission of information is useful to those who think they can make money in milliseconds, it is of only limited purpose for those with a long-term outlook and the knowledge that too much of a good thing, at least in this case, is too much.

Yes, Warren Buffett actually does have a Twitter account. But, no, he doesn't rely on it to make money. Neither should you.

9

Fear the Fed

"IF SOMETHING CANNOT GO on forever, it will stop." Known as Herbert Stein's Law, the maxim is just one of many contributions Stein, economic advisor to presidents Richard Nixon and Gerald Ford, made to twenty-first century investors. For the 30-Minute Millionaire, however, the idea that unsustainable conditions ultimately will be just that—unsustainable— is a vital bit of truth. Moreover, Stein believed that when an unsustainable condition persisted, there was no need to go to extraordinary measures to make it stop, as it would die of its own accord once conditions were no longer favorable. For our purposes, the theory speaks to the fundamental changes we are going to witness and serves as a cornerstone for this book's premise: extreme levels of financial market support that have persisted since 2008 cannot go on forever, and the coming years will see that support collapse under its own weight. In short, times are changing, and we all have to be able to change with them.

Now, this does not mean that doom and gloom lie ahead after years of market prosperity. To the contrary, the American growth engine is likely to keep humming along strongly enough to prevent a major recession or an exceedingly painful, prolonged downturn in the capital markets. Indeed, despite what we see as significant headwinds on the horizon, investors will still be able to make money. Doing so, however, is going to become more challenging. The days of money-pumping stimulus are behind us; the era of the wily investor who understands that opportunities will present themselves in some unlikely places is just getting started.

In a nutshell, the "something" that "cannot go on forever" is the reckless fiscal and monetary policies that have prevailed during most of our young century. Runaway budget deficits, the arbitrary throwing of money at "shovel ready projects," and trillions of dollars in money printing by the Federal Reserve are over. No matter how much these practices helped pump up asset prices and shield Americans from the underlying truth of their slow-growth economy, they cannot continue. Left unchecked, the high budget deficits would lead to crippling inflation. Ditto for zero interest rates and endless easing at the Fed, which also comes with the added penalty of mass asset misallocations. What has gone on for years cannot, and will not, continue.

What does this mean for investors? There will likely be a future of consistently lower returns compared to what we saw with the beginning of the bull market in 2009. In the six years that followed, the S&P 500's average annual return was about 17.4 percent, or nearly 50 percent higher than its typical return going all the way back to 1928.[1] At this point, you might say that such a big run would be expected when coming out of a crisis like the one that hit our financial system during the subprime mortgage collapse, and the violent reaction that followed. But these market gains didn't come amid a bustling economy—quite the contrary, in fact.

Gross domestic product, the value of all goods and services produced in the US, never broke 2.5 percent on an annualized basis during the entire recovery period.[2] Taken all together, the recovery, such as it was, has the dubious honor of being the worst since the Great Depression. The bull market, though, is one of the strongest in history: in March 2015, on its sixth anniversary, it ranked as the sixth longest of all time in duration and fourth-strongest in terms of percentage gains. Something is clearly not right here. So what is it? This chapter is going to explore that very question.

To do so, we're going to take you on a ride through the recent history of the Federal Reserve's monetary policy. If you want the short version, the importance of this exercise to your core portfolio is that we recommend against buying long-term bonds and believe that stock market investing is going to require more savvy than in past years. The longer version is more complicated. It involves the manipulation of markets by a central bank that believed it was charged not with merely controlling inflation and employment, but rather goosing financial markets to a create a "wealth effect" that was supposed to benefit all Americans. We believe it's important not merely to understand what you're doing, but the underlying reasons why as well. We are also cognizant, however, of the core belief we are imparting here, which is that none of this should occupy excessive amounts of your time. So if Fed policy isn't your thing, you can simply save this chapter for another day and move on to the next topic. For those interested in the mechanics of the future market, however, please read on.

The most important stock market development in the post-crisis world has not been the surge in corporate profits, modest economic growth, or any of the other usual suspects one would look for in trying to discern equity gains. Rather, the market's best friend has been the Federal Reserve. Though the Fed was set up to help govern the banking industry and determine monetary policy, in recent years it has been on a mission to inflate asset prices. Amid the depths of the financial crisis, the US central bank embarked on a policy that will likely change the way we look at market behavior permanently.

In 2008, while the market looked like it was in a free fall and the economy seemed ready to drop into a funk that rivaled the Great Depression, the Fed stepped in with the most aggressive monetary policy moves the world had ever seen. In an effort to quell investor fear and get consumers and businesses to start spending again, the Fed embarked on a bonanza of rate cutting and money printing. It began slashing rates with a half-percentage point (50 basis points) cut in September 2007 and dropped rates twice more that year. In 2008, it dropped rates seven more times, including two cuts in October in the days after Lehman Brothers collapsed. The Fed didn't stop until December, with a frantic 0.75–1 percentage point cut that took the target funds rate to as near zero as possible.

The Fed funds rate is critical on a number of levels. In the most tangible sense, it is used as a peg for multiple other rates throughout the economy, including how much interest is charged on credit card purchases, the kinds of return savers get on their bank accounts, and the rates companies have to pay to borrow money. In a less tangible sense, the rate sends a signal to the economy, in which the Fed says with its rate moves, "Here's where we think financial conditions are, and here's how tight or loose we think lending standards should be." With that series of actions, taken while it looked like the financial world was about to end, the central bank's Open Market Committee sent an unmistakable message to America that it was time to loosen up.

Not everyone listened, though. Stung by the freewheeling days of the early twenty-first century housing boom, and facing intense pressure from Washington, banks essentially shut off the spigots no matter how low interest rates plunged. With plenty of justification, banks were tasked with shoring up their balance sheets and increasing their cash positions so that a

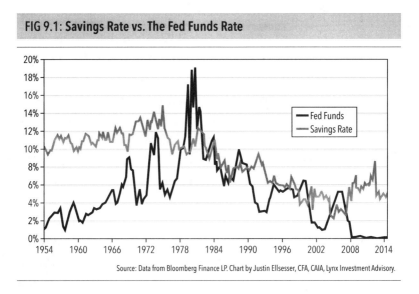

FIG 9.1: Savings Rate vs. The Fed Funds Rate

Source: Data from Bloomberg Finance LP. Chart by Justin Ellsesser, CFA, CAIA, Lynx Investment Advisory.

crisis of the magnitude that hit the world in 2007–2009 would not be repeated.

Consumers, meanwhile, protected their own rear flank. After years of their own kind of recklessness—taking out "liar loans" that required no documentation of salary or credit history and running up mountains of credit card debt—regular folks buckled down. Looking at the 10-year period from March 2005 through March 2015 is instructive when examining consumer behavior. The personal savings rate bottomed out at 1.9 percent in July 2005 amid the go-go real estate market. When the Fed began cutting rates in 2008, the savings rate was still at a relatively meager 2.8 percent.[3] As rates cascaded, those plain-vanilla savings accounts and money market funds became increasingly losing propositions. So when the Fed funds rate fell to zero at the end of 2007, that really should have pushed those misers into action, and into the kind of risk-taking the Fed was trying to stimulate. Except it didn't.

With savings returns stuck on zero, savers themselves doubled down on their conservative behavior. The savings rate climbed from 2.5 percent in November 2007 to 7.9 percent in May 2008, despite the Fed regime's intentions. A year later the rate spiked again, to 8.0 percent. Over the next three-and-a-half years, the savings rate never fell below 5.0 percent. In December 2012, it spiked to 10.5 percent and by March 2015 it was at a still-elevated 5.3 percent. So despite the Fed's most strenuous efforts, it had decidedly limited success in kindling those fabled animal spirits among the American consumer.

So if consumers and mom-and-pop investors were sitting on their hands during this time, who or what was pushing up the stock market? The unfortunate answer to this question gets to the really pernicious effects of Fed policy.

You see, there were two parts to the central bank's recipe for getting the economy going again. The first consisted of what we've discussed so far—a maneuver financial market insiders have come to call zero interest-rate policy, or ZIRP. The second goes by a variety of names. The most technical, and the one Fed officials most commonly use, is Large-Scale Asset Purchases (LSAPs). Another less formal term has been adopted by economists trying to explain the program—"quantitative easing," or the common abbreviation "QE." For our purposes, those two letters help explain, better than virtually anything else, the market's meteoric rise off its financial crisis lows.

At its heart and in theory, QE essentially involves the Fed stepping into the private market for bonds—mostly government (such as Treasuries) and quasi-government issues (primarily from Fannie Mae and Freddie Mac)—and becoming a player. The program allows the Fed to buy bonds that financial institutions accrue, a move that, in turn, provides those institutions with liquidity that they then can deploy in the type of activities that spur economic growth. To execute its goals, the Fed gets to do something we all wish we could do when we'd like to get our own personal wheels rolling again during slack times: it gets to create money. You may have read in the papers or seen financial experts talking on TV about the Fed "printing money." In truth, it doesn't actually print anything. Instead, it just credits its own account with digital funds, which it then passes along to the holders of the various securities it buys. So while there's not any actual new *physical* currency floating through the system, the effect is essentially the same. Nice work if you can get it.

There's an added theoretical benefit to QE as well: the Fed's involvement creates demand for those bonds, thus driving up their face value and pushing down their yields. And, as a game show host might proclaim, that's not all. Those low bond yields are supposed to push investors who gravitate toward ultra-safe US government debt elsewhere. Indeed, as the Fed puts it in a QE primer on its website, the quest for yield would send those investors scurrying "to acquire assets with higher yields—assets such as corporate bonds and other privately issued securities."

The Fed was right. Plunging bond yields sent some investors groping for assets that offered more, and pushed others into the risk markets for products like stocks, and, to a lesser extent, commodities, such as energy and precious and industrial metals. But the overall effects on growth were nowhere near what the Fed had projected. For, as we know, reality often turns theory into fantasy.

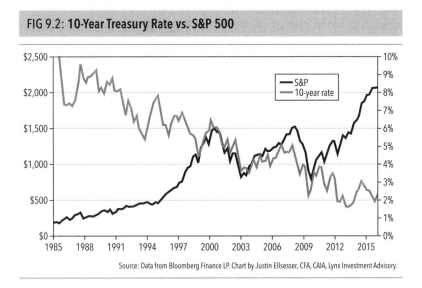

FIG 9.2: **10-Year Treasury Rate vs. S&P 500**

Source: Data from Bloomberg Finance LP. Chart by Justin Ellsesser, CFA, CAIA, Lynx Investment Advisory.

The chart in Figure 9.2 shows the imperfect relationship the stock market and interest rates have had over the years.

In its QE primer, the Fed claims the overall effect of the LSAPs was to "put downward pressure on yields of a wide range of longer-term securities, support mortgage markets, and promote a stronger economic recovery." Indeed, rates fell sharply across the board. The 10-year Treasury note, considered a benchmark figure for the bond market and economic growth, yielded 4.5 percent the day the Fed enacted its first crisis-era rate cut. Interestingly enough, yields drifted higher in the immediate aftermath, but that soon changed. As 2007 progressed, yields began to slip, eventually ending the year hovering around the 4.0 percent level. In 2008, a series of aggressive rate cuts put further pressure on yields, keeping the 10-year solidly below 4.0 percent through much of the year, then below 3.0 percent by the time November rolled around.

By this time, though, the market had changed. Trading volumes on the major stock market exchanges were drying up, and mom-and-pop investors moved to the sideline, pushing the balance in plain-vanilla money market accounts past $4 trillion. Those that were left in the market, however, decided they liked having the Fed around. The first iteration of quantitative easing—QE1, if you will, from December 2008 to March 2010—saw the S&P 500 stock market index surge more than 28 percent. In the Treasury market, though, things didn't work out exactly as planned. The 10-year yield actually climbed as the Fed was scooping up Treasuries, jumping from 2.37 percent around the start of QE1 to 3.84 by the end.

As you'd perhaps expect, the phenomenon reversed itself when the Fed took its foot off the accelerator. When the first round of QE ended, the stock market almost immediately went into a tailspin. From April until mid-August, the S&P 500 kept sliding until it put on the brakes just short of bear market territory—a 16 percent decline that showed Mr. Market had become a quick addict to the financial drug the Fed was pushing. With stocks about to enter their first bear market phase since the financial crisis, central bank officials moved to take decisive action. What followed would make history.

Call it financial engineering, the beginning of the new era of central banking, or the day the Federal Reserve jumped the shark. On August 27, 2010, then-Chairman Ben Bernanke gave one of the most pivotal speeches in Fed history. Addressing the group of central bank officials, economists, and guests gathered at the Fed's annual retreat in Jackson Hole, Wyoming, Bernanke made it clear that going forward the organization would no longer focus solely on what had traditionally been the two-pronged, or dual, mandate of maximum employment and price stability (i.e., keeping a lid on inflation). No, the Fed chief asserted, the organization now would become stewards of the US economy. They would not merely hold interest rates low enough to keep the jobless rate in check and make sure the cost of living didn't get out of control, but also goose the financial markets by taking whatever steps necessary to provide liquidity and assure investors the Fed would be a backstop for both the financial system and capital markets. The pivotal part of Bernanke's Jackson Hole statement was this:

> The Federal Reserve is already supporting the economic recovery by maintaining an extraordinarily accommodative monetary policy, using multiple tools. Should further action prove necessary, policy options are available to provide additional stimulus. Any deployment of these options requires a careful comparison of benefit and cost. However, the Committee will certainly use its tools as needed to maintain price stability—avoiding excessive inflation or further disinflation—and to promote the continuation of the economic recovery.[4]

There simply was no room for interpretation in what Bernanke said. In broad terms, the chairman made it clear that the Fed was going to continue providing support to keep the plodding economic recovery going. Wall Street, though, put a finer point on it. Just months after ending an unprecedented program to help a nation in crisis escape the worst downturn in three quarters of a century, the Fed was preparing to launch a second phase—QE2, as it quickly became known. The "Bernanke put" was firmly in place, and the market was ready to take off.

On September 24, hedge fund star David Tepper—who to that point had kept a fairly low profile as he built his Short Hills, New Jersey-based Appaloosa Management up to $12.4 billion in assets under management—made a big splash on national TV. Speaking during a segment of CNBC's "Squawk Box" program, Tepper boiled down what Bernanke's comments ultimately would mean for the market: "Either the economy is going to get better by itself . . . or the economy is not going to pick up in the next three months and the Fed is going to come in with QE. Then what's going to do well? Everything in the near term, though not bonds . . . " Concluding his assessment of Bernanke's positioning, Tepper said, "You talk about when you get moments. This might be one of those."

So began what market watchers whimsically started calling the "Tepper rally" (created largely by the "Bernanke put"). That day the S&P 500 gained 1.5 percent and would shoot 11.0 percent higher in total by the end of the year. In November, the Fed announced what everyone knew was coming—the second round of QE, this time with the intent to "print" another $600 billion in a program that would run until the following June. The equity markets were off and running. Of course, the only thing that could stop the rally was the end of QE2, which indeed came the following June, marking the momentary interruption of another Fed-induced rally. On July 7, 2011, a week or so after the end of QE2, the S&P 500 peaked at 1,353.22 then began a harsh slide quickly thereafter. By the time the damage was done in early October, the index tumbled 19 percent, again just missing a bear market, and sent up another distress signal that the Fed was only too happy to answer.

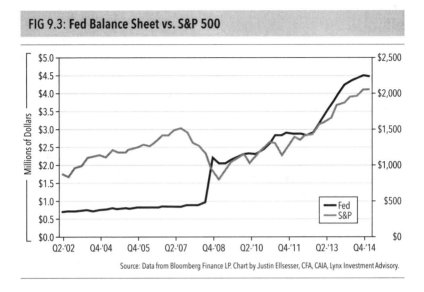

FIG 9.3: Fed Balance Sheet vs. S&P 500

Source: Data from Bloomberg Finance LP. Chart by Justin Ellsesser, CFA, CAIA, Lynx Investment Advisory.

On September 21, 2011, the Fed concluded its meeting by announcing a new program called Operation Twist. This time, the Fed would continue buying bonds, but it wouldn't be printing any additional money. Instead, it would simply buy longer-term bonds and sell shorter-term ones, with the intention of driving down longer-term rates and extending its portfolio duration. Markets rallied, and the Fed liked what it saw. Emboldened by the apparent success of its previous programs, in September 2012 the Fed doubled down, and then some, on the previous versions of QE, announcing an "open-ended" program that the markets ultimately dubbed "QEternity," or "QE Forever."

The point was that our central bankers would no longer accept the constraints of "quantitative" targeting of balance sheet expansion or an arbitrary calendar date that limited its ability to conduct operations. Now, the Fed would simply intervene in financial markets for as long as it wanted and deemed necessary.

After QE, QE2, Operation Twist, and QE3, the tally was stunning: the Fed's balance sheet had expanded to more than $4.5 trillion in money created out of thin air that helped propel a stock market rally of more than 200 percent. It had been seven years since the Fed stepped in after the crisis, and zero interest rates still ruled the day. Though the Fed enacted its first rate increase in more than nine years in December 2015, it will likely be years before the central bank cuts loose the apron strings—or choke-hold, depending on your perspective—that it attached after the financial crisis clobbered the US economy.

We relate this back-of-the-cocktail-napkin history of recent Fed activity for an important reason. Keep in mind the quote with which we began this chapter: "If something cannot go on forever, it will stop." History has shown us that extreme monetary easing conditions cannot go on forever. Therefore, the Fed will stop. When it does stop, investors like you will have to pick up the pieces.

It's a fair question at this point to ask why the Fed continued its policies well past their apparent expiration date. Chairman Bernanke was the pivotal member of a three-person body, colloquially known during the financial crisis as "The Committee to Save the World." Along with Treasury Secretary Henry Paulson and New York Fed President Tim Geithner, Bernanke helped mastermind a potpourri of programs that helped the financial system recover from the devastation the crisis brought to the US and global economies. All of those programs that helped recapitalize and restore faith in the nation's banks, such as the Troubled Asset Relief Program (TARP), were temporary. One was not. You can guess which one.

But why were all those other programs allowed to expire? The reason the others are no more is because they were crisis-level moves meant to address a crisis. So, too, were QE and ZIRP. Yet the Fed has chosen to continue its nursing of the financial system, even well beyond the effective end of the crisis. TARP, for instance, allocated enough resources to get banks back on their collective feet, then cut the cord. The logic was simple: while it was important to restore the system's health, it was equally important to make sure banks understood that they couldn't go running to the Treasury every time they had a capital issue. QE and ZIRP, however, came with no such strings attached. The Fed has essentially pledged that each time the financial markets enter a swoon, the central bank will crank up the virtual printing presses.

One clear manifestation of this pledge has been the woeful misallocation of capital in the era of Federal Reserve largess. In a 10-year period running through mid-2015, US companies spent $4 trillion buying back their own stock—a staggering spending spree that occurred while retail investors dedicated a net of just $100 billion into the equity markets.[5] Corporate America has been playing a fun game using money borrowed at bargain-basement rates to buy up their own shares, boost their share price, and give their members sweet bonuses based on this increase in share price.

Since the crisis, earnings per share numbers have looked stellar in large part because there are simply fewer shares, meaning stock market multiples have gained even if actual top-line revenue increases at an anemic pace. As far as actual investment in growth-producing activities like new plants and new employees, that can wait for another day. Aside from a short-lived post-recession spike of 12.9 percent in 2010, real gross domestic investment has lagged, registering a historically meager 4.9 percent gain in 2013 and 5.8 percent in 2014[6]—numbers that are even worse when you consider the Fed injected nearly $4 trillion in fresh liquidity to the system since the advent of its QE program.

In addition to propping up stock market prices, the Fed's policy did indeed push investors into higher-yielding choices. High-yield bonds—you know them by their more common sobriquet "junk"— attracted huge sums of investor money. Companies with the worst debt ratings were able to raise money at historically cheap rates—around the 6 percent range for much of the ZIRP era. Total junk debt issuance hit a nominal record of $334 billion in 2013, or nearly eight times as much as at the depths of the financial crisis in 2008. Total corporate debt issuance, excluding non-convertible debt, topped $1 trillion for each of the years 2010–2014, with investment-grade issues peaking at $1.43 trillion in 2014.[7]

This arrangement between the Fed and the stewards of the US economy is messy and unnecessary—the consequences of which nobody really understands yet. Don't tell that to the Fed's counterparts around the world, though. They've seen the big gains for the US stock market, overlooked the anemic economic growth, and decided to follow the same path down the road to easy money. The Bank of Japan, which failed miserably in its first small-scale stab at QE back in the 1990s, launched its own program under the direction of Prime Minister Shinzo Abe. As a cornerstone of his "Abenomics" program and its "three arrows" to spur economic growth, Japanese-style QE had predictable results: a big leap in the stock market, with the Nikkei 225 index jumping nearly 19.0 percent in the first five months of 2015, but less success elsewhere. Japan's GDP grew just 0.5 percent in the fourth quarter of 2014, when the new iteration of QE began, and a meager 0.3 percent as recently as Q3 of 2015. The results were even worse for inflation, which Japan has desperately tried to goose after a generation of deflation. In the face of a program that was printing money at an annualized rate of up to 70 trillion yen, the equivalent of US $712 billion, the inflation rate was flat six months after Abe released his QE arrows.

In Europe, the results of QE have been equally unbalanced. The FTSE 100 Index outpaced the American stock indexes in the first half of 2015, but it came as euro zone economic growth couldn't eclipse 0.4 percent, with crippling debt continuing to weigh on growth in the region. Across the world, other central banks were tripping over each other to devalue currencies, print money, and push the belief that a soaring stock market was a reliable proxy for a robust economy.

For the 30-Minute Millionaire, the takeaway from seven years of extreme easing is fairly simple, despite its complex machinations and repercussions—follow the printed money, but watch your back. In the years ahead, the US central bank is going to be zigging while its global counterparts are zagging. The Fed was years ahead in terms of seeing the benefits of zero interest rates and endless money printing. It will now spend the coming years dealing with the consequences. Interest rates will begin rising, while financial conditions tighten. Will the Fed be able to resist QE4 if the markets can't handle higher rates? Others including the ECB, BoJ, and others around the world are unlikely to be deterred by dangers unseen, so don't expect them to take the foot off the pedal anytime soon.

That will set up some interesting choices. The US markets—for years the benefit of a slew of silly metaphors like the cleanest dirty shirt, the best house in a bad neighborhood, and "TINA" (There Is No Alternative)—will struggle to capture investor dollars. As developing markets mature and other alternatives become more prevalent, US equities could become also-rans.

Everywhere on Wall Street people say, "Don't fight the Fed." We tell you to fear the Fed. This august institution—which did so much to restore faith in the US financial system and, in general, calm the waters after the financial crisis devastation—became too enamored and too confident of its role and has stayed around much longer than needed. Its actions were once a vital balm to a system that had lost the faith of investors, regulators, and the public. Now it has created a level of uncertainty in the system, the ramifications of which are still hard to gauge. Even to its top officials, it is unclear how the Fed will unwind a $4.5 trillion balance sheet and stage manage a rise from seven years of zero interest rates. For investors, and the 30-Minute Millionaire in particular, dangers lurk.

As we all know, however, dangers bring opportunities, which we firmly believe can be unearthed in just 30 minutes a week.

10

The 411 on 411

WE **LIVE IN THE** Information Age, or so we think. We're awash in information—data, analysis, and opinion—all of it converging on us daily from our smartphones, mobile devices, desktop computers, televisions, and radios, gadgets and implements that permeate our lives to provide whatever we want to know at a second's notice.

But do we really need it all? Ralph Waldo Emerson once said, "There are many things of which a wise man might wish to be ignorant." The quote could serve as an effective epigram for this book. On many levels, today's investor is suffering from information overload. As in all other aspects of the media landscape, there is now a 24/7 news cycle in the business world. Cable television and the Internet combine for an as-it-happens potpourri of financial news, from the data point of the moment—China manufacturing, euro zone GDP, US nonfarm payrolls, you name it—to the latest big company news or whipsaw trading movements. It's hard to believe that only a generation ago, most folks away from Wall Street had to read the morning paper or at least watch the six o'clock news to find out how the market did on a particular day. It's harder still to believe that few people cared. Once upon a time, most investors designated a set share of their money to the market and checked back in on it every once in a great while. Today, more and more average folks are making knee-jerk decisions based on the news of the moment. This is one of the principle trends our book is trying to counter.

Some of the things you read in this chapter might strike you as a bit funny considering one of our authors. Jeff Cox has been with CNBC since 2007, most recently as the finance editor and a frequent TV guest where you can watch him conveying the latest news, as well as occasionally getting into a little animated cross talk with other experts on the network. So let's just dispense with the obvious right off the bat: we think you should watch CNBC. We think you should read CNBC.com and use it as one of your prime sources of financial world news. The important point we want to make is about *how* you process information from CNBC and all the other financial news sources out there.

The key to the whole process is to consider what you're getting from these sources to be "information," in the strictest sense of the word. While many TV folks, journalists, bloggers, and the like may offer what appears to be "advice," we believe you should process it as "information." Francis Bacon didn't say, "Information is power." Instead, he said, "Knowledge is power." Information is what we know. Knowledge is what we do with it.

A well-read and well-versed investor is highly likely to make better decisions than someone who takes stock tips from a cabdriver. As we've said before, knowing why you're doing something is as important as knowing what you're doing. We want to encourage you to take in good information where you can find it, then use that information to make sound, long-term decisions that meet your investment goals and risk profile. We want to discourage you from making decisions based on information in a vacuum, selling based on one good or bad piece of economic data, or buying because you've heard three prognosticators on TV tell you that Company A is the next big thing on the market.

To be sure, there are some investors who can trade the market and do well, though most fail. CNBC and other media feature these winners on a regular basis, and we respect many of the folks who are out there with their sleeves rolled up in the market every day, making short-term decisions and profiting handsomely. If you wish to join their ranks, we wish you well and hope you thrive, too.

Now, with the ground rules laid out, let's take a look at the information on the information. What's ahead is a list of the best places to get data, analysis, and opinion. You may have a few of your own. These are a few of ours, with all of the lists in no particular order.

On the straight news side we'll round up the usual suspects: *The Wall Street Journal, Financial Times, Investor's Business Daily, USA Today's* money section, and the business section of the *New York Times* should be on your list. For the global wonks among you, add *The Economist* as well. There obviously are too many publications to mention individually in this category, but these are the top ones, in our view.

If you've gone through this book and been baffled at a few points by the terminology, then first, let us beg your pardon. We've tried to use as plain language as possible. Second, go either to Investopedia.com or Investorwords.com. Both sites are excellent for helping decode the dense, jargon-filled world of investing and finance. In that regard, we've also discussed exchange-traded funds at length in this book. The best site out there for following the latest trends in these critically important instruments is, not surprisingly, ETF.com. There's not only a wealth of data on the site but also commentary and analysis from the very best minds in this $2 trillion, and rapidly growing, industry.

Let's dig a little deeper now.

In the opinion and blogger realm, there are lots of smart folks out there in the financial world with many interesting and important viewpoints. Unfortunately, there are a number of charlatans with an agenda out there as well. In the blog world, just a few we'll mention as worthy of your consideration. (Disclosure time again: Jeff Cox edits a blog called "NetNet" for CNBC.com. We think it's pretty good.) One is Josh Brown, aka The Reformed Broker. Josh, a CNBC contributor, is both a trader and a guy with a long-term perspective on the market who actively tries to dispel the folly of conventional wisdom. Find him at thereformedbroker.com. You also should put the *New York Times'* "DealBook" in the rotation. The feature is edited by Andrew Ross Sorkin, who's also a CNBC host. Finally, your reading day, every day, should include a visit to "Morning Market Briefing" by Nick Colas, the chief market strategist at New York-based brokerage Convergex. Quite simply, Nick provides perspective and analysis that you just won't find anywhere else.

There are a slew of sites that blend news, snarky opinions, and occasionally entertainment. A few of our favorites are Dealbreaker and Business Insider. There also are those that fall in the aggregator category—essentially sites that scan the digital world for news and pull the headlines together in one place, with direct hyperlinks to the respective stories. The two best in this category are the Drudge Report, of course, and RealClearMarkets.

Overall, the blogosphere offers thousands of financial blogs and sites from which to choose. A few years ago, Insider Monkey made a list of its top 100, which is still useful, although some of the blogs on the list don't exist anymore. Access it at insidermonkey.com/blog/best-finance-blogs-199748/ and make up your own mind. As for data and other more straightforward sources for information, we'll hit on a few that will help you keep perspective on where the financial world is heading.

The Federal Reserve's site offers a plethora of data points. If you want to get inside the central bank's mind and read up on its latest decisions, the place to go is federalreserve.gov/newsevents/

press/monetary/2015monetary.htm. The latest speeches from
Fed officials are here: federalreserve.gov/newsevents/speech/
2015speech.htm. (Both of these pages have dropdown menus
where you can search through their archives.)

To keep track of the more granular parts of the economy, there
are a multitude of sites you can visit. The most important economic release each month is the nonfarm payrolls report. You
can access it at bls.gov/cps/. If you're a data geek and really want
to get inside the jobs numbers, you can go to data.bls.gov/cgi-
bin/surveymost?ln where you can get historical data on virtually
any employment data point you'd like. Our favorite is http://www.
bls.gov/news.release/empsit.t15.htm, where you can find the real
unemployment rate (i.e., the one that includes those people who
have quit looking for work and are working part-time for economic reasons). While the government was touting an unemployment rate that was just 5.3 percent in mid-2015, this alternate
measure showed the real rate to be 10.5 percent. Getting a clear
picture of our economic health is important.

The data points you get from the government, though, are
often unreliable indicators of true economic health. For instance,
it's pretty hard to take it seriously when we're told that the most
reliable way to gauge inflation via the Consumer Price Index is to
exclude energy and food prices. Ivory tower economists will dis-
miss those two categories as being "volatile" and their movements
"transitory." Kind of a silly way to look at things, don't you think?

In all, information can be your friend but some of it, particularly that which delves into opinion and forecasting months or
years into the future, also can be your adversary. In our previous
book, *Debt, Deficits, and the Demise of the American Economy,*
we implored folks to use epistemic thinking in approaching your
views on the world and your subsequent investing decisions. That
means taking a fact-based, linear look at what's before you and
avoiding prognostication and guesswork. In short, please keep
Mr. Emerson's words in mind.

11

Listen to the Gurus

A WORD OR TWO FROM co-author Jeff Cox:
Over the course of a journalism career that began in 1987, I've been blessed to have met, and made long-term connections with, some of the top investing minds in the business. You have heard of some of them, but other names won't be familiar to you. It's an odd world I've experienced, covering Wall Street. Some of the folks my peers and I consider rock stars won't get the attention of many readers. After all, we're not, generally speaking, out there trying to get exclusives with George Clooney, LeBron James, or Taylor Swift. Instead, we chase the latest investing advice from David Tepper, Nassim Taleb, or Nouriel Roubini. You probably have heard of Warren Buffett; you may not know Jim Paulsen. I may not be able to tell you about the time I hung out with Mick and the Stones in Rio (where they once played to 1.5 million fans), but I can brag that I once had a beer with Jamie Dimon in Davos.

Jamie Who? Where? For the uninitiated, he's the straight-out-of-central-casting CEO at JPMorgan Chase, and Davos, Switzerland is the site of the annual World Economic Forum—both very big deals in my world.

These connections are a very good thing for you, the reader who's trying to find the way to becoming a 30-Minute Millionaire. A few of the very best minds in the business were kind enough to sit for extensive interviews relating to their views about the investing world and how things are likely to shake out in the years ahead, along with the very premise of the book, which is that you do not need to, nor should you, spend more than 30 minutes a week on your investing portfolio. Some of their views are not entirely in-line with ours, but we agree on most of their major premises, and their thoughts are valuable.

This chapter features several interviews with a select handful of these great minds. Regular watchers of CNBC and other business channels should recognize their names. The format will be mostly question-and-answer, so you have the opportunity to hear their unvarnished words of wisdom. A word of caution: at times the discussions will veer a little deep into the weeds. We denizens of the investing world can get a little wonky sometimes, and it's perfectly understandable if you don't find some of the details all that compelling. In other words, feel free to browse. Peter and I, however, strongly feel that it is important not to just understand what is going to happen, but why.

We start with one of the brightest minds in the investing world, Mohamed El-Erian, the chief economic advisor at Allianz—a global financial services company with nearly $2 trillion in assets under management. Mohamed also is the former CEO at Pimco, the California bond giant where he coined the term "New Normal." He first publicly uttered the term during a CNBC interview amid the darkest days of the financial crisis. The New Normal became a widely used description of the slow growth the world faced ahead. Today, Mohamed remains a regular presence in the financial media, including his widely watched appearances on CNBC and in his writings for the *Financial Times*. He also was once thought to be on the short list for the Egyptian prime minister. We're glad he stayed in the financial world!

Jeff Cox: Mohamed, investors have been dependent on central banks, specifically the Fed in the US, to provide a low-volatility, high-return environment. However, we know that can't last forever. How do you think this all plays out, and how should retail investors adjust?

Mohamed El-Erian: So you raise several issues. The first one is the macro, the second is the impact the macro has on the pricing of markets. The third one is the cost of repositioning in today's global markets. Three distinct issues.

If we take them in that order, on the macro side, my strong view is that we cannot continue on the path we're on and expect that it will remain a low-volatility path. If you look forward over the next three years, there are things happening that make it very difficult for central banks to control volatility.

The first that's happening is divergence of policy. You have the Fed slowly easing its foot off the accelerator, while you have the ECB (European Central Bank), the Bank of Japan, and China that not only have their pedal to the metal but are actually looking to press it even harder.

This speaks to a main concern about the path that we're on. We are going from uniform policies to divergent policies. That of course speaks to divergent economic circumstances, different parts of the cycle, et cetera.

The second is that central bank policies are becoming increasingly ineffective because the gap between financial risk-taking, which is high, and economic risk-taking, which is low, is getting bigger.

What do I mean by that? Economic risk-taking is the willingness of companies to invest in new plants, equipment, and people. Because there is genuine medium-term uncertainty—and because of the nature of the innovation cycle, which is a winner-take-all innovation cycle—companies are becoming very hesitant to invest. What you have had is a big gap, and there's a good reason for that.

If you're a company looking to invest in plants, equipment, and people, you have to take five years. If you are an investor, you believe you can change your mind tomorrow. So we have a big gap between economic risk-taking which is low, and financial risk-taking, which is high . . .

The final reason is political. We are seeing in Europe, we are seeing in this country, a growing reaction to what my Pimco colleagues and I called the "New Normal." It's a world in which inequality gets to be a bigger issue politically. If you put these three things together, it is very difficult to maintain the current scenario.

JC: How does it all end, though? We've never seen central bank intervention on this scale, so it's pretty hard to say what's going to happen when they pull the plug, right? What happens when the liquidity investors have come to depend upon goes away?

ME: The result is the "T" junction. Over the next three years, the path that we're on now, which is central banks repressing volatility, is going to end and either we're going to tip into a good equilibrium because we get into a critical mass of good things, or we're going to tip into a bad equilibrium, which is low growth and financial instability.

When it comes to translating it to what happens in markets, the markets love the journey because the journey has been incredibly profitable. The reason why it's been incredibly profitable is there's lots of liquidity sloshing around in the system. When companies are hesitant to invest in plants, equipment, and people, they accumulate cash on their balance sheets. When they accumulate huge amounts of cash on balance sheets, they are under incredible pressure from shareholders to release it . . .

That results in three things: one is higher dividend payments, two is higher share buybacks, and three is higher defensive mergers and acquisitions. All three tend to support the equity market, so in the short term all these really interesting macro things are going on. The market focus is going to be on cash, which means that the market is unlikely to adjust to the macro till quite later.

If it's coming out to the "T" junction, and we turn into the good equilibrium, that's fine because that's a world in which better fundamentals validate high financial asset prices. If, however, we take the other turn then there will be a major adjustment. My probabilities for these two things are relatively the same. I don't like saying that. There simply isn't enough evidence which turn will dominate at this point.

The third point is repositioning. The marketplace is in love with the illusion of liquidity. It's not just an illusion, it's become a delusion. There is a conventional wisdom in the marketplace that when the paradigm changes, the markets collectively will be able to reposition relatively smoothly. But as we have seen repeatedly in the last two years, starting with the taper tantrum, including what happened in the German bund market, when the paradigm changes, liquidity becomes very elusive. As an investor you want to have optionality. You want to be able to develop your thinking and your positioning.

JC: So how should investors protect themselves against all these risks without having to spend excessive amounts of time and energy on their portfolios?

ME: As we get more information, as we get closer to the neck of the "T," that's a fundamental issue. Different people do it in different ways. The way I like best is the barbell portfolio, which is you reduce your exposure to the most heavily trafficked markets, which are the public markets. You take some of that and put it in cash, which gives you optionality for the future. But you don't totally give up on the upside. You put it in higher-risk areas that are less trafficked— venture-type elements, competing markets in developing countries. You find that a number of smart hedge funds are doing that now . . .

When I look back, the mistake I made was not to link the economic concept of the New Normal to the willingness of the [central] banks to become more and more unconventional.

JC: The Fed seems to have taken on a third mandate in addition to full employment and cost stability and now is basically trying to manage the entire economy, and the markets, correct?

ME: There's nothing surprising about it if you go back to [Bernanke's] August 2010 speech, which really marks the pivot the Fed made from targeting the normalization of markets. QE1 was about normalizing markets. QE2, which was introduced by Bernanke in August 2010, was about economic objectives. If you go back to the speech, he had that wonderful phrase, when you go QE you have to remember the "benefits, costs, and risks," and the longer you stay in this unconventional policy, the greater risk, or the greater the probability that the benefits will go down relative to the costs and risks.

The question is, what are these costs and risks? A lot of the other stuff that you have written about from the potential of excessive risk-taking to the politicization of central banks to income distribution issues—there's a lot of things that come into play. Bernanke, whenever he is confronted with this, he acknowledges there's risk there, but [he says they are balanced by] the big economic growth we're going to get.

JC: You raise so many important issues. What we're worried about, and what we're trying to accomplish with this book, is to convince folks to stay invested but not to overthink all of this. Is that possible?

ME: Now you're raising a fundamental issue, which is that people increasingly are focusing on the short term. Some people are forced to do so because the costs these days of underperforming can be quite high, because money moves pretty quickly. So whether you are a mutual fund or whether you're a bank, you become much more sensitive to the short term.

That's one issue that has occurred. That's why you get a lot of people who say I know that valuations are rich if not expensive, but then I'm willing to wait till I have evidence . . . because the policy has been continuously for central banks to come in and support the market.

You have investors that have now been conditioned to buy on the dips . . . Why? Because people truly believe the central banks are both willing and able to suppress financial volatility.

It's one thing when central banks are going the same way. It's harder when they are divergent.

It can be either. That's why I think of the concept of the "T" junction. It can work. We can look back and celebrate that central banks got the game going until other policy makers got their act together.

They never handed off to a more holistic policy response. The private sector took too much financial risk relative to what it can do on its own. The things that bothers me the most, Jeff, is I would love to be able to tell you that this side dominated the other side. There's nothing I would like better to have the conviction, and the foundation, to be able to say this is what is most likely to happen. Unfortunately, there's simply no evidence that speaks to one side of the "T" dominating the other at this stage.

It's one in which the most critical question for investors is: "How much are you willing to give to maintain optionality?" Central banks are making it very, very hard to maintain optionality because they're taking interest rates to ultra-low levels. They don't want you on the sidelines, they want you to take more risk, they want you to raise asset prices. They hope by doing so they will trigger the wealth effect. You open your 401(k), it's going good, you spend more money, and that, in turn, triggers the animal spirits of companies.

That's what they hope. They don't want you on the sideline.

———————————

Next up on our expert panel: Jim Paulsen, chief market strategist at Wells Capital Management in Minneapolis, which has more than $350 billion under management. Jim, too, is a fixture of the business journalism world, known for his plain-spoken views on the markets and the economy. It would be fair to call him an optimist—he is a firm believer in America as a global leader and his advice most often directs clients in some way, shape, or form to US equities. In 2015, however, Jim turned more cautious. He saw a US market that was getting a little rich and a Federal Reserve that waited too long to hike rates. The Fed should have been doing so when corporate earnings were on the rise, rather than wait until 2015 when the profit cycle was beginning to flatten.

Jim Paulsen: I don't think we'll get through it without some turbulence. We're in the mother of all monetary easing cycles. To think that we're now going in to turn the monetary boat for the first time and we're just going to ride right through, it just seems a little bit unrealistic to me.

The Fed has waited too long to start this process. That's not to say that they're necessarily behind the curve. They could be, but that's not my concern. Generally, when you look back when the Fed initiates a tightening cycle, it does it against a very definitive buffer. The buffer is that the profitability cycle is still recovering.

People take comfort and say there's a lot of periods where the rates went up and the market did OK. But every one of those periods were because profits were still recovering. We waited too long to start. The traditional exit ramp off strong profitability has expired, so the Fed's got to do this without the ultimate buffer, and I think that's a bit of a problem. If we were at 16 times earnings, I'd feel a little different. I just don't know.

JC: Does that mean that there will be better opportunities outside the US?

JP: The US is unique in the world in that it's one of the few places that's nearing overheat pressures. Nobody else is in that position—nobody else is talking about when they're going to raise rates. Why not get away from that when we're dealing with that in the initial stages and move to other parts of the world that are in a different place?

Japan, the emerging world—which is probably going to sustain a growth rate over the next two years and next generation that is twice the rate that is sustainable for the developed world—last year gave you an opportunity to buy commodity-based stock markets because the deflation scare emerged. Canada and Australia got beat up mightily by last year's oil drop. This year that's going the other way. The dollar is going to go back down this year, not up.

As far as sectors, in the US the exposure I'd have now is more inclined toward the cyclical side. What I would do with the market is barbell my exposure—some cyclical, energy, materials, and industrials. For the most part all have underperformed but have been at the bottom on a relative basis. I'd subsidize that by overweighting two defensive sectors.

I would tend to underweight both the darlings—healthcare and discretionary. Energy costs are going to go back up, rates are going to go up. I would still be equal weighted in much of the rest—tech, financials also have small-cap bias globally.

Consequently, Jim believed the road was being paved for an inflationary atmosphere that the Fed would have a hard time combating, thus leading to low, if any, returns for the year. As of this writing, Jim's words proved prophetic. Stocks struggled through the first half of 2015 as investors worried over what the Fed would do and how it would normalize policy.

Perhaps more importantly, though, for the purposes of our book, Jim brightened when I brought up the concept of the 30-Minute Millionaire—specifically that investors can spend too much time on their portfolios.

JP: The vast majority of your portfolio, you probably literally should take sort of a once a year approach towards it. Set it in motion and revisit once a year. If you just can't stand that, then give yourself a small portion of your portfolio that you can play with during the year. If you screw that up, it won't screw up your overall portfolio. At least it gives you enough chance to stay sharp.

I would suggest once a year you set an allocation relative to your long-term parameters. You either don't really visit that for another year or you set up intervals where you automatically revisit it on a formulaic deal: if rates do that, I'll make this change. If these stocks do this, I'll make this change. I would revisit it every quarter and then try to make up your mind on things. I'd try to make that more for once a year decisions.

I think you can be too involved sometimes, including even guys like me. Sometimes our worst enemy is we just came into work today and, because of that, we make decisions where we would have been better off if we didn't bother to come in.

Very experienced people in the business do the same thing. We're all guilty of that to some extent. I imagine it's even harder for those doing things less than once a day. There's some truth in that things don't move near as fast as advertised or as you think they should. There isn't often that big of a change that creates that much opportunity as you might think.

There's a big difference between staying engaged, and staying sharp and abreast, and making decisions. That doesn't mean there's anything wrong with staying engaged, but you also need to have a process through which you're going to make decisions. Those are different things. You certainly don't want to make them at a cocktail party where you're talking to your buddies.

From her perch atop the strategy team at Charles Schwab, Liz Ann Sonders boasts one of the most respected voices in the world of finance. Calling her one of the most influential women on Wall Street misses the point—she's one of the most influential people, period. You'll recognize Liz Ann from her appearances on financial TV broadcasts as well as the recurring role she had on the Louis Rukeyser version of "Wall Street Week"—a show she had watched to get her own education about the investing business.

One of the things I like most about Liz Ann is her distaste for "forecasting," something Peter and I railed against in our previous book. She doesn't, for instance, engage in the pointless practice of giving annual forecasts of some imaginary number as to where she anticipates the S&P 500 might land by the end of a given year. Instead, she focuses on directionality and the general strength or weakness of respective capital markets. In 2011, she did tell investors to start buying equities, right at the point that the market had bottomed for the year. It's no accident, then, that she commands the respect she does, and it's our privilege to include her words of wisdom as the final thoughts from our panel of experts.

JC: One of the basic concepts of this book is that we foresee investment returns heading higher but not at the pace we've seen in the post-crisis market. How do you see things playing out?

Liz Ann Sonders: I would agree with you for several reasons, certainly on the fixed income side. With the onset of the rate hike cycle, which will be slow compared to other rate hike cycles, rates are still going up. They won't be going up in staircase style like we saw with the last cycle, so I don't think it's a stretch to say that returns on the bond sides of your portfolio won't be the same as we saw in the 1970s.

We're probably in an area where you get a greater amount of choppiness—kind of a grinding higher versus basically the six straight up years that we've had. I look at a variety of valuation metrics, including Shiller's CAPE [discussed in chapter 7]. I've also written things that critique Shiller's CAPE. I think it provides fairly intelligent guidance.

Using that as a proxy for what we might expect, yes, you should expect lower equity returns, lower fixed-income returns. I think we are in a secular bear market for commodities. Better put, we are no longer in the super-cycle for the upside of commodities. What happens is when you exit the super-cycle you go through an elongated period of overall flatter performance for commodities, with a level of choppiness. We think the commodity super-cycle ended in 2011, and I don't think a new one starts anytime soon.

When you start stacking those things together, when you look at a broadly diversified portfolio, it doesn't mean investors are not going to have opportunities within random asset classes, but we do need to temper our expectations for returns.

JC: Those low expectations are kind of what's keeping the bull market going, right?

LAS: Absolutely. I think return expectations are very tempered. I don't think there's anywhere near the kind of enthusiasm . . . it certainly hasn't been euphoria on the part of the retail investors. It's been basically a corporate buyback driven stock market. That's one of the reasons why I think the bull market is ongoing.

JC: Another trend we see playing out is the end, at least for a while, of the traditional 60/40 portfolio allocation of stocks to bonds. Is that what you're seeing?

LAS: I think that's already happening. There's a reason for the success of what we call "robo-advice." Certainly Schwab is

involved in it now. I think it's more about a general obser-
vation around not only the need to be diversified, but also
the need to be diversified into asset classes that are non-correlated, that could provide opportunities relative to stocks,
bonds, cash, traditional allocation models.

JC: As far as investing vehicles go, mutual funds still have the
greatest total of assets, but ETFs are quickly catching up.
Does active management still have a place for investors?
(Note: Schwab is the seventh-largest issuer of exchange-
traded funds, with about $35 billion under management as
of mid-2015.)

LAS: The growth in ETFs is obviously greater than the growth
in traditional mutual funds.

I happen to think we're in an era right now where there are
opportunities for more active managers. That said, when
you're talking about individual investors, more often than
not, individuals are probably better served to taking a passive approach to indexing things to the S&P 500. Anything
that continues to support that trend I think is positive.

JC: So you're in favor of a barbell strategy, with most allocated
to indexing and some toward riskier moves?

LAS: One of the big mistakes I think a lot of pundits make,
even if they're representing their own firms, is to answer
questions like that with a cookie cutter answer or go back to
what are perceived to be tried and true methods.

It really is a function of your risk tolerance. One of the big
mistakes that investors make is they directly tie risk tolerance to time horizon. They assume or set up a portfolio
that is on the riskier end of the spectrum. If they're younger,
and have decades to retirement, they automatically bucket

themselves in that aggressive camp. If that same investor is going to freak out and panic and capitulate and sell at the first 8 percent drop in the market, I don't care how long their time horizon is—that's not a risk-tolerant investor.

We talk about the rear view mirror and performance chase. We also say turn the mirror to yourself and understand who you are as an investor, what are the things that are going to trip you up. True risk tolerance is, "How much can my portfolio decline before I make a really dumb decision and panic and do something that turns out to be a really wrong decision?"

JC: How do you feel about the US versus the world?

LAS: This could be a short-term thing. Right now, we have a neutral recommendation across the three broad global equity classes: US, developed international, and emerging market. We at Schwab don't have a bet in any one region. Will there be opportunities, possibly even in the near term, where you want to have more exposure? The underlying message for a lot of investors who have been very biased toward the US is you want to make sure you have global diversification.

JC: The change in dynamics between global central banking, with the US easing while the rest of the world tightens, has to present some global opportunities. How does that play out?

LAS: The theme of the last several years had been convergence. The Fed was first out of the blocks. We were in this loosening provision of liquidity and now we're taking the first steps toward monetary policy divergence. The biggest economy is moving in a direction opposite of what the ECB, the Bank of Japan, and the Bank of China are doing. Do I think we're in a longer-term influence of central banks? Yes I do.

Never, ever fight the Fed, or fight central banks; they can pull us out of any hole we find ourselves in? That view is a little bit scary. Not that I oppose the notion of "don't fight the Fed." I still believe in it, but I worry sometimes the market assumes there's this perpetual central bank put.

We won't know until we get out of this perceived uncertainty. I'm enough of a skeptic, I try not to wear rose-colored glasses, and believe that you just don't fight the Fed and don't fight central banks in perpetuity and you'll be great.

JC: So what keeps you up at night? Is it the Fed, is it the global economy, or is it something else?

LAS: I'm a chronic insomniac, so I'm up every night. Who knows, it could be something as simple as a shopping list or it could be [being the parent of] teenagers. When I get the question as it relates to the market, I wonder just how massive what we've seen central banks do, what the downside is to it. We can easily argue about mispricing. You can't help but wonder if we get to some point where we look back and say, how did we not see this coming? You can't go back in history [and say] the last time the Fed took its balance sheet to $4.5 trillion here's what happened.

JC: One of the ideas behind this book is to dispel the idea of short-termism, that you can time this market and play the game the traders play. How big a worry is that to you?

LAS: There was a big attempt and push to do that in the 2010 and 2011 time frame when we had the flash crash, and high-frequency trading was dominating trading volume. I know this anecdotally—they felt that the only way to play that game was shorten time horizons and take more of a timing approach. Our message back then was you should do the opposite.

Don't try to play the game of traders and trade in nanoseconds because it's a losing proposition for investors. If anything, you want to lengthen your time horizon when others are shortening theirs.

JC: Should investors be picking individual stocks?

LAS: There are investors who love it. They love having skin in the game, they love the process of researching. I would never say every investor, don't bother picking stocks, just index or hire a money manager. But if you're going to do it on your own, you have to do the work. I really do think that even if you're self-directed, reaching out for advice is important. It's more accessible than it's ever been, at a lower cost than it's ever been. We should afford ourselves the opportunity to access great advice and think of our financial lives more holistically.

JC: So for the retail investor, who maybe doesn't have the time to do all that legwork, is it possible to manage it all in 30 minutes a week?

LAS: It depends on the investor. If you're a self-directed investor, you have to put a definite amount of time in, you can't wing it. But if you're using an advisor, a private client advisor, you want to be engaged, you want to be informed, you want to have a partnership with that advisor. But that's when you don't want to second guess and obsess about every monthly return in your portfolio. Really, that's very much a personal decision. But there are probably more investors that are self-directed and making investments on their own, that should actually be more passive investors, than there are passive investors who would do a better job of it on their own.

12

Understanding Risk

MOST OF US HAVE our own understanding and view of risk. We tend to think of activities, decisions, and even internal thoughts as safe or risky, or somewhere in between. In other words, we attribute degrees of risk to activities or things. We'll all agree that there is risk in investing in stocks because we know that stocks don't just go up. When they go up, we make money; when they decline, we lose money. That's the risk we take.

But can we measure and quantify the risk in investing in the markets? A great deal of academic thought and theory has gone into answering that question. (We discussed risk in a chapter of our previous book, *Debt, Deficits, and the Decline of the American Economy*. It may be worth a look if you're interested in a more in-depth discussion of the history of risk. Some of our comments here are adapted from that chapter.) Let's look at the types of risk you should understand when we talk about investing.

When you flip a coin, what are the odds it will come up heads or tails? You know the answer: 50 percent. So if you flip a coin 100 times, tails will come up 50 times and heads will come up 50 times, right? Most of us also know that it might work out that way, or it might not. If you try the experiment, you'll end up with many different results. Heads may come up 60 times and tails 40 times in one case. Or, in another, tails might come up 58 times and heads 42 times. The greater the number of flips, though, the greater the chance that the end result will be close to 50/50.

Now, what if in the course of our little experiment heads comes up eight times in a row? What are the chances heads will come up on the ninth flip? (Casino aficionados will recognize this conundrum as the red and black phenomenon on a roulette wheel: if red comes up eight times in a row, do you bet on black during the next spin?) The answer, of course, is still 50/50. The coin you are flipping is not blessed with a memory. It doesn't know that it came up heads eight times in a row. The odds on the next flip are still 50/50.

We are talking about flipping coins to introduce the subject of probability. Interestingly, throughout history probability theory was slow to get off the ground. The ancient Greeks didn't have much use for it, nor did they spend much time on it during the Renaissance. Yet every insurance company must deal in probability theory to price a life insurance policy, or any other kind of insurance. After all, those companies need to have some idea of the odds of when those people they've insured will die and how much they'll have to pay their heirs. Probability is a function of mathematics, so most of the work done in this field is credited to great mathematicians.

Let's introduce Carl Friedrich Gauss, who was born in Braunschweig, Germany in 1777. Among Gauss' greatest achievements, and the one of primary interest to us, is his use of the "bell curve." (The bell curve was originally developed by a French mathematician, Abraham de Moivre, some 80 years before Gauss was born.)

Somewhat counter-intuitively, the bell curve is used not to determine accuracy, but rather to determine error, and by how much. When you invest in stocks, you might expect to earn a 10 percent return over the years, but since you can't forecast that future return accurately, what you really want to know is how far off your return might be from the expected 10 percent. That is what we mean by "error." Now we are into the study of probability.

For example, you are planning a vacation trip to Hawaii next month. What are the chances it will rain a lot during your trip? If you take a bus trip to Chicago in July, what are the chances the bus might crash? Would you be safer in an airplane? What are the chances of a stock market crash? The bell curve and Gauss offered an answer. Even if you've never heard of the term "bell curve," you may remember talking to your fellow students in high school or college about an exam that was going to be "graded on the curve."

Bingo! That was the bell curve. And Figure 12.1 is what it looked like.

Grading on the curve simply meant that your teachers or professors were not going to assign a specific grade for each exam

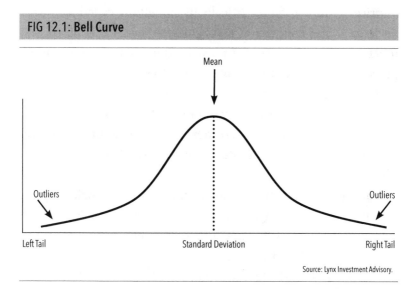

FIG 12.1: Bell Curve

Mean

Outliers

Outliers

Left Tail   Standard Deviation   Right Tail

Source: Lynx Investment Advisory.

based on how many right answers each student got. Instead, if a test was particularly tough, and most of the class did poorly, they might decide to use the curve, which meant distributing the grades around a mean, or an average. So even if all of the results on a given test were lousy, the teacher would give an average grade, say a C+, to the ones that were average for the entire group of papers, and then distribute the rest of the grades around that average grade, or mean. So the ones who were better than the average would get a higher grade, and the ones who were worse would get a lower grade. That meant that even if you didn't do well on the exam, but if you did better than everyone else, you got an A.

The bell curve shows the distribution of a number of different phenomena or events. Let's talk about stocks. If you consider buying a hi-tech company stock that has a historic range of prices over the last five years between $4 a share and $125 a share, we would all agree that that particular stock is volatile. A different stock, perhaps that of a public utility, may have only fluctuated between $20 and $30 over the same period. Clearly, the utility stock is much less volatile than the hi-tech stock. The changes in price are measured statistically by something called "standard deviation." The majority of stocks don't move up or down that much, and indeed those that move around the least represent 68 percent of the total sample of stocks. That 68 percent group is said to be within one standard deviation of the mean. So 95 percent of the stocks are within two standard deviations, and 98 percent are within three standard deviations. Using this scale, you can easily see that standard deviations greater than three are rare events indeed.

Consider another type of distribution: average male heights. Assume that the average height of men in the US is 5'8" with a standard deviation of 2 inches. That means that 68 percent of men are between 5'6" and 5'10" tall. Ninety-five percent of men are between 5'4" and 6'0" feet tall; that's the two standard deviation measure. Now we get into rarer territory: three standard deviations. At this level, the men range between "shorties" of 5'2" and tall fellows of 6'2". The distributions continue on both ends of the bell curve with increasingly rarer results, from little people to NBA centers.

Why is this important? There are many reasons. Take the following case: suppose you are a rich manufacturer in China that doesn't know anything about the US (except that it buys a lot of your little widgets) and you want to take your family on a vacation to America. Good weather is an important consideration, of course. You will be traveling in February. You ask for the average temperature in various US locales and your trusty assistant who hasn't travelled much comes back with two places, Minneapolis and Honolulu, each with average temperatures around 74 degrees. That'll do, you say. And you had better hope you didn't pick lovely Minneapolis in February for your trip. How can both cities have the same average year-round temperature? It's all in the distribution.

Put another way, Honolulu has a very low standard deviation of temperatures, while Minneapolis has a very high standard deviation. The range of year-round temperatures in Honolulu is from a low of 53 degrees to a high of 94. In Minneapolis, the range is much greater: from a low of –34 degrees to a high of 105. And guess when the –34 degrees is likely to happen? That's right— during your February vacation. In any event, we have Friederich Gauss to thank for the use of what is now known as the "Gaussian Bell Curve" to measure these distributions, a statistical process that is still very much in use today.

We suspect some of you may be asking how knowing all this will help you succeed in managing your 30-minute portfolio. It's all about understanding and managing risk. Many inexperienced investors tend to seek out the investments with the highest historic returns. For example, with your handy laptop computer, you can screen for funds or even stocks that have had the best performance over the past 3, 5, or even 10 years. Why not just buy the funds that have performed so well in the past? Because, and you've heard this before, past performance doesn't guarantee future success. Sure, but doesn't a history of good performance tell us something about the skill of the manager or the attractiveness of this particular area of the market? Indeed it does. But if that fascinating manager you're thinking of investing with is also among the most volatile, watch out. We're talking about the mistakes many investors made during the Internet bubble market in 1999 and 2000.

Here's a classic. In December 1997, Ryan Jacob starting managing the Kinetic Internet Fund. Under his management, the fund soared 196 percent in 1998, and then banked another 216 percent gain in 1999. And the money flowed in. The fund went from $20 million in assets to $1.2 billion in 24 months. At that point, in December 1999, Jacob decided to start his own fund—Jacob Internet Fund. Investors rushed to subscribe. You probably know what happened next. The bubble burst. A $10,000 investment in the Jacob Internet Fund at its inception was worth less than $500 two years later. This is, to say the least, a perfect example of the effect of risk, plus a few other Biblical lessons thrown in, like greed and hubris.

So understanding and respecting risk is very important. And since you can't predict the future, you need to look for telltale signs of risk before it hits you over the head. As in the examples you have just seen, high volatility is one sure sign. A fund that can go up 200 percent in one year can come down pretty fast, too.

Does this mean that you should avoid risky assets in your 30-minute allocation? Not at all! It does mean that you should apportion risky assets appropriately. Some asset classes, like emerging markets, are more volatile, and hence riskier, than the more established market in developed countries. That doesn't mean you don't want to own emerging market stocks. It means that you should allocate a smaller amount of money to this particular area than you do to the more stable countries, simply because it is riskier.

Another way to mitigate risk is through an understanding of correlation. A well-balanced portfolio has asset classes that do not correlate well together (correlation is discussed at length in chapter 7). What this means is that you don't want all of your different investments to go up and down simultaneously. A well-correlated portfolio will help you withstand the erratic behavior of the stock market and lessen the trauma of violent market moves.

Here's an example. Correlation is measured as a value between −1 and +1. Let's say you own two different large-cap funds in your portfolio, managed by different managers. You might think you've diversified your investments, but you really haven't. Since both managers are buying the same types of stocks, those of large companies, their correlation is likely very tight. What is a high correlation measure? Any number between 0.7 and 1.0 (which indicates perfect correlation). Indeed, a correlation of 1.0 means that your two funds are likely to go up and down in lock step.

The correlation between stocks and bonds is, as you might know, low. Stocks and bonds don't go up simultaneously—a portfolio that owns stocks and bonds is said to be diversified. In terms of correlation number, a 0 value (on the scale of −1 to +1) means there's no correlation—the two asset classes behave independently. What about a negative number? A negative correlation, like −0.5, suggests that the two asset classes go in opposite directions. Take gold. Having gold in your portfolio will help diversification. When stocks are doing very well, the gold price will likely lag or go down, but while in a crisis, stocks may well decline and gold may well soar. That's negative correlation, and it also helps to diversify your 30-minute portfolio.

Here's what you should remember from our brief discussion of risk. Risk in investment portfolios cannot be eliminated. You simply have to understand risk, limit it as much as you can, and live with the consequences. To limit risk intelligently, you will diversify your investments to lessen wide swings in value that may affect both your finances and your nerves. You should respect volatility and understand that as volatility rises, risk often rises, too. Armed with your awareness of the power of risk, you are now better prepared to build your portfolio with confidence.

13

Getting Rich over Time: Show Me the Money!

IT'S TIME TO PUT the title of this book into practice and show you how to make a million dollars in 30 minutes a week. That's what we promised; now it's time to deliver.

We are using three sets of assumptions. It's not likely that any one of these will match your exact situation. Use the one that comes closest to your individual circumstances. Here they are:

- **Portfolio 1** has a starting amount of $10,000; it assumes monthly contributions of $200 for the first 5 years, then contributions of $400 a month for the following 5 years, and contributions of $550 a month for the remaining 30 years.

- **Portfolio 2** has a starting amount of $50,000; it assumes monthly contributions of $300 for the first 5 years, then contributions of $500 a month for the following 5 years, and contributions of $1,000 a month for the remaining 30 years.

- **Portfolio 3** has a starting amount of $120,000; it assumes monthly contributions of $750 for the first 5 years, then contributions of $1,200 a month for the following 5 years, and contributions of $1,500 a month for the remaining 30 years.

Each of these assumed starting points involve an initial investment, then continuing investments over the years. We have attempted to be realistic in creating these three levels. In our experience, they represent a range of dollar investment that will encompass the vast majority of readers. These are the different levels of estimated monthly or annual contributions you will make as you save toward your retirement or other goals for the money you will amass. For those of you who are, very intelligently, starting to invest in your early twenties or early thirties, we project your earnings out to as much as 40 years. In most cases, you'll achieve the goal of a million-dollar portfolio long before that time, as you'll see. Later on, we'll show you how each of these portfolios should grow over time.

We will now add another variable: the kind of portfolio you will adopt based on your personal risk preferences. Normally, we speak of conservative, moderate, and aggressive portfolios. We are not using the conservative model here because we are dealing with long-term investment objectives, where a moderate or aggressive strategy will be appropriate even if you encounter severe market turbulence along the way. The main factor to consider is your ability to withstand this inevitable market turbulence. If you will lose sleep over periods of market weakness, periods that could last months, then the moderate portfolio is a better choice for you. Otherwise, if you have more than ten years before your retirement, or a different objective for your wealth, and you accept that there will be periods of weakness over time, you can opt for the aggressive portfolio.

That's it.

Now we want to show you some of the tools used in the investment consulting process. These are fairly sophisticated tools based in part on Modern Portfolio Theory and the work of notable economists and investment trade practitioners. It would be easy enough for us to concoct a portfolio and tell you how such a selection of stocks, bonds, and other investments will ensure your million-dollar, or more, retirement fund. But why would you believe us? Instead, we want to familiarize you with some of the more advanced tools used in the investment world to predict future performance of your portfolio. Understanding these tools will help provide you with the confidence that your goal is realistic—knowing that will help you stick to it.

Think about why these tools are so important. Most institutional investors—the people who run college and university endowments, charities, and foundations—all have one thing in common: a need to create income for their institutions, scholarships, grants, charitable obligations, and the like. More importantly, they need to do so reliably, since most of their obligations are commitments they have made in the past. Since most of them are invested in the stock market, which is inherently unpredictable in the short to intermediate term, they need tools to back up their investment decisions and ensure that the money their institutions need will be available when they need it.

We know, and the professionals know, that you can't predict the future. We don't know when the next bull market will start or end, we don't know when the next crash will occur, and we don't know when the next crisis—financial, political, or otherwise—will happen. The best thing we can do is play the odds. That is why the finance academic community came up with a strategy, with an admittedly curious name for a serious financial application: Monte Carlo simulations.

In its simplest form, the Monte Carlo analysis tries to answer the following question: given how your portfolio is allocated among different asset classes (stocks, bonds, commodities, etc.) what kind of return can you expect over time? To answer that question, we look at all the variables from the past. The Monte

Carlo crunches all the numbers of the past performance of every asset class in your portfolio, based on the market indexes for each asset class, to determine how it performed under different conditions throughout history. The analysis does this for each asset class, then it puts them all together and runs different scenarios thousands of times to see what might happen if all of these asset classes did well over the next 5 or 10 years—and what would happen if they all did miserably over the same time period. The Monte Carlo also figures out what the portfolio might look like with various combinations of these returns at any given time.

You can correctly surmise that these are massive calculations requiring extensive number crunching that only the most powerful computers can accomplish. Indeed, it was the advent of large computing power that made these simulations possible.

So what does the Monte Carlo analysis tell us?

It tells us this: given your existing portfolio, and everything we know about how your different asset classes performed in the past, the most likely return for your portfolio over 5, 10, and 20 years is, say, 8 percent.

OK. That's the most likely return. You get it. But what if you don't get that return for whatever reasons? What else might happen?

Fair question. You see, the Monte Carlo simulation will not only give you the most likely return, but it also will tell you what your potential return will be if conditions are not among the most probable. In that case, your portfolio will do better or worse than the expected return. And the calculated range will cover about 90 percent of all possible outcomes.

"That sounds more reassuring," you say. Indeed it is, which is why many professional investors use these simulations to predict their future performance. In this book, you will, too. Have a look at Table 13.1.

This table shows the results of a Monte Carlo simulation representing the expected return, and the *range* of returns, for the moderate and aggressive portfolios we are proposing in this book.

TABLE 13.1: Monte Carlo Simulation: Return Forecast				
		Percentile		
95th	75th	50th	25th	5th
1 Year				
Aggressive 37.55	18.09	7.32	-2.21	-15.16
Moderate 29.06	15.09	6.91	-0.77	-10.68
5 Year				
Aggressive 20.53	12.71	7.60	3.03	-3.12
Moderate 16.90	11.0	7.04	3.55	-1.26
10 Year				
Aggressive 16.65	11.30	7.82	4.42	-0.51
Moderate 13.78	9.84	7.23	4.61	0.94
20 Year				
Aggressive 13.75	10.20	7.71	5.35	2.20
Moderate 11.73	9.01	7.12	5.37	3.02
30 Year				
Aggressive 12.68	9.69	7.68	5.66	3.04
Moderate 10.95	8.63	7.11	5.61	3.59
40 Year				
Aggressive 12.02	9.33	7.60	5.93	3.44
Moderate 10.39	8.41	7.08	5.82	3.96

Source: Morningstar

In the aggressive portfolio, the range of gains and losses is wider because we are taking more risk. That means that when times are good, you'll make more money with the aggressive portfolio than with the moderate portfolio. When times are bad, however, you'll lose more money with the aggressive portfolio than with the moderate one. In a word, the aggressive portfolio is riskier.

Note that the table covers periods of 1, 5, 10, 20, 30, and 40 years. Also note that as time goes by, the range of returns becomes narrower. That's because, over time, we expect the returns to more closely parallel their long-term historic performance. Accordingly, our confidence in getting those returns increases with time. Let's have a closer look at the table.

The 50th percentile is the average expected return over time. This is the return that will be most reliably produced over the years. As time passes, your confidence in getting those returns will increase. So, look at the one-year return for both portfolios. The range of returns is wide! Sure, in any given year you could have a major bull run in stock prices or a major crash in the market. But crashes don't happen every year, nor do stocks go up in a straight line for years. So as time goes by, the range of returns narrows.

But looking at the one-year range for the aggressive portfolio, we see that our *expected return*, the middle case or 50th percentile, is 7.32 percent. The *range* of returns for any given year, however, goes from a *loss* of 15.16 percent to a *gain* of 37.55 percent. These statistics are based on history and statistically encompass 90 percent of all probabilities. In other words, there's a 5 percent chance the bottom could go lower and a 5 percent chance the high could be higher. For all practical purposes, it encompasses 95 percent of probabilities, since we don't really mind if we're wrong on the upside (that would be the year the portfolio does better than 37.55 percent!).

For the moderate portfolio, the expected return for any given year is 6.91 percent. The range of returns in any given year goes from the 5th percentile return, really bad conditions with a loss of about 11 percent, to the 95th percentile return, really great conditions with a gain of about 29 percent. The 10-year expected return for the moderate portfolio is 7.23 percent, while the 10-year range goes from about 1.0 percent a year at the 5th percentile to the happy return of about 13.8 percent at the 95th percentile.

Look at the range of returns of the two portfolios over time. Over 10 years, the aggressive portfolio at the 5th percentile might have earned nothing and had a small loss of less than 1 percent a year if conditions were really bad. At the opposite extreme, with the 95th percentile, you would happily be contemplating a 10-year annualized return of more than 16 percent—an unlikely, but possible, event. Spend some time reviewing this table. Browse through the range of returns for both the moderate and aggressive portfolios to see which one might best suit you.

In this chapter, you've learned about some of the techniques used by professional investors to predict the returns on the portfolios under their custody. Hopefully, knowing these techniques instill in you the confidence that the returns you expect are likely to occur if you just have the patience to stick with it over time, and to monitor your investments sensibly, in, yes, just 30 minutes a week.

In the next chapter, we'll delve deeper into how these portfolios are constructed and what assumptions you can use to forecast your future returns.

14

Building the Portfolio
(Part 1)

BY NOW YOU HAVE decided between a moderate and aggressive portfolio, and you have reviewed the three potential starting dollar amounts (shown in chapter 13), along with the accompanying monthly contributions. It's not likely that any of the three examples will match your circumstances precisely, but that's not important. The figures represent a range of outcomes, one of which should be close to your own circumstances, and that's the one to follow. The dollar figures we use won't mirror your exact situation; they are used as examples of how these different amounts can enable you to reach your objective of one million dollars or more.

In the previous chapter, we showed how professional investors use Monte Carlo simulations to give them the necessary confidence that their objectives will be met. These estimates start with a set of assumptions. We call these "capital market assumptions."

TABLE 14.1: Capital Market Assumptions		
	Return	Standard Deviation
Small Cap Domestic	9.90%	21.58
Large Cap Domestic	5.98%	15.42
Domestic Fixed Income	5.83%	5.75
Emerging Market	10.11%	25.41
International Equity	5.00%	17.95
Gold	11.64%	21.27
Energy	11.15%	22.90
Real Estate	15.79%	21.98
International Sovereign Fixed Income	5.22%	7.32
All Cap Alpha Manager	11.00%	23.41

Source: Morningstar

They are shown in Table 14.1 for the various asset classes we will be suggesting you hold in your portfolio.

Note that for each of these asset classes, we list an estimated return. These estimates are the historic returns going back 15 years. They cover the major market declines in 2000 and 2001, following the collapse of the Internet bubble, and the stock market collapse in 2008–2009 in the wake of the financial crisis, the worst since the Great Depression. The period also covers the stock market recovery following the 2008–2009 major declines. By using historic returns, especially those that include two major market setbacks, we take the guesswork out of using a future return number based on our, or someone else's, best guess.

You'll see another column to the right of the "Return" column: this is the standard deviation for each of these asset classes. Standard deviation is a measure of risk. (We discussed risk and how it is measured on Wall Street in chapter 12.) For now, just remember that a high standard deviation indicates a riskier asset class—a lower one indicates less risk. Not surprisingly, the riskier asset classes offer a higher return as compensation for the risk you're taking. And it could go the other way. If conditions deteriorate, you will likely lose more money with the riskier asset classes than with the less risky ones. That is why asset allocation is so important. A well-constructed portfolio needs to balance the risks.

As you browse through the different asset classes in the list, you will recognize most of them. You may be less familiar with the two asset classes at the bottom of the list. One is "International Sovereign Fixed Income." This asset class offers a good balance of reward and risk. It includes investments in bonds of foreign countries where the bonds are guaranteed by the respective governments. Of course, some countries are safer than others, and it takes painstaking analysis to determine which countries and their bonds make the best investments. This is yet another reason why we believe investment decisions should be made by experts. In this case, we'll recommend a mutual fund or exchange-traded fund that has a good track record. Also note that, in most cases, the bonds of these foreign countries are denominated in US dollars, thereby avoiding currency exchange risk. Note, too, that we emphasize short-term bonds for the amount of your money we propose for fixed income. We believe that interest rates will begin a long rise, in which case existing long-term bonds will decline in value. (See chapter 9, "Fear the Fed.")

The other asset class at the bottom of the list is "All Cap Alpha Manager," which will sound like gobbledygook to most nonprofessional investors. "All cap" refers to stock market capitalization, the value of any particular company in the market place. We generally divide stocks by size into "small cap," "mid cap," and "large cap." "Large cap" refers to large companies with recognizable names such as GE, IBM, Google, Facebook, and of course, the largest of them all, Apple. "Mid cap" and "small cap" are alternatively lower in value.

Most managers and funds specialize in one of these three size categories. When we use the term "all cap," we are saying that the mutual fund or money manager isn't restricted to one particular size and can pick stocks in any size category: small, mid, and large.

"Alpha" refers to a Wall Street term that denotes market out-performance. A manager who consistently performs better than the pertinent stock market index is said to create "alpha," or excess performance. When we want an All Cap Alpha Manager, we are saying we want to select a money or fund manager who can beat the market returns and who is not restricted to any specific company size or market capitalization. Why is this a special asset class? Don't we expect all of our managers to beat the market? If only . . .

We've learned through time that very few managers can consistently beat the market (see chapter 5). In most cases, you should opt for market returns and the much lower costs they entail. But you also want to reserve a special place in your portfolio for a talented manager who you believe has a good chance, and a record to support it, of beating the market. These managers tend to have concentrated portfolios, choosing only a few stocks they have come to know and love. A concentrated portfolio, however, is inherently riskier than a large portfolio. With a large portfolio, a disaster at one company, resulting in a plummeting stock price, will have little effect in a portfolio that might have several hundred other stocks.

There are 10 asset classes included in our portfolio model. You may be surprised to see so many different investments, especially since we expect you to track them in only 30 minutes a week! This wide-ranging mix of managers and funds will be the best way to diversify your portfolio and spread the risk around. Moreover, given the advent of ETFs (see chapter 6) there are many opportunities today to invest in asset classes that, until recently, were not available to any but the largest investors. We intend to take advantage of their availability to help you diversify your portfolio and provide additional opportunities for good performance and lower risk.

How Much Do You Put in Each Asset Class and Why?

The right question, and perhaps the single most important investment decision we ever make. Many investors have been told that asset allocation is the most important factor in explaining investment performance. Indeed it is.

Where you put your money is much more important than who is managing it. Here's an example: the Japanese stock market peaked in 1989 when its Nikkei index hit 38,915. Since that year, the index hasn't come close to that level again. At this writing, the Japanese market has been on a bull run, but it is still selling at around one half its 1989 value! So imagine you're invested in Japan and you are lucky enough to have the hottest money manager or fund manager working for you—the Peter Lynch or Warren Buffett of Japan, perhaps. It won't do you any good. They'll be investing in a market that peaked 25 years ago, so even with substantial outperformance above the index, you will be losing money. In other words, the decision to invest in Japan was far more important, and damaging, than the decision of what fund or manager you may have picked. Because of this, the asset allocation decision will be the most important consideration in our 30-minute weekly exercise. We'll write more specifically about it in chapter 18, dedicated to how we spend time in our 30-minute sessions.

The allocation we propose for these portfolios is designed to create the best balance of risk and expected returns. These allocations are not sacrosanct and some investors will want to tinker with them according to their own preferences and risk tolerance. Remember, the higher standard deviation allocations are the riskiest, while the lower standard deviations are the least risky. If, for example, you want your portfolio to be more conservative than the ones we suggest, reduce allocations from the high standard deviation investments in favor of those with lower standard deviation. Please remember, however, that these portfolios have been carefully designed to optimally balance risk and return. You can likely adjust these allocations slightly to your own preferences, but we do not suggest drastic changes to what we have recommended.

The proposed allocations for the aggressive and the moderate portfolios are shown in Table 14.2.

These allocations are categorized by asset class. You'll need to populate your portfolio with specific investments—in most cases mutual funds, ETFs, or index funds. We'll help you do that later on. From a practical standpoint, the smaller portfolios won't be able to buy as many as 10 different funds or ETFs since many funds (although not ETFs) have minimum investment sizes that may be $2,000 or more. For the small starting portfolios, we'll recommend funds that combine two or more of the recommended asset classes.

TABLE 14.2: Proposed Allocations for Aggressive and Moderate Portfolios

Asset Class	Aggressive	Moderate
Small Cap Domestic	15.00%	10.00%
Large Cap Domestic	17.00%	20.00%
Domestic Fixed Income	8.00%	25.00%
Emerging Market	15.00%	10.00%
International Equity	14.00%	10.00%
Gold	3.00%	5.00%
Energy	0.00%	0.00%
Real Estate	10.00%	5.00%
International Sovereign Fixed Income	3.00%	5.00%
All Cap Alpha Manager	15.00%	10.00%

Source: Morningstar

Where Do You Keep Your Investments?

You'll want to open an account at a low-cost brokerage firm such as Schwab, Fidelity, or E-Trade. There's no reason for you to use a full-service brokerage firm with a securities salesperson or to pay higher fees than those at the discount brokers, where most trades can be done for under $10. Another important feature is that many of the low-cost firms provide added features, including an automated analysis of your portfolio holdings, pie charts showing your diversification by type of investment, and unrealized profits and losses on your investments. Many of these features will be helpful in the periodic review of your investments (and we'll thank these firms for helping keep your investment analysis to under 30 minutes a week).

In some cases, you won't have the luxury of keeping all your investments in one place. Some of you will participate in 401(k) plans at work, and those assets will likely be in custody elsewhere. That's not a big problem, though. Just keep track of which investments are at which firm, and when it comes time to review the investments, have the statements from both firms handy. If you participate in a 401(k) plan, the investment choices likely will be restricted to that firm's choices. This shouldn't be a problem since any firm administering a 401(k) will offer a range of index funds, and you can just as easily use theirs in your investment allocation.

15

Building the Portfolio
(Part 2)

IN PREVIOUS CHAPTERS, YOU'VE seen how we put together portfolios that are intelligently diversified to spread the risks around. In chapter 14, we chose 10 asset classes that we recommend for your long-term portfolio. We also offered specific allocation percentages for each category, and we introduced the Monte Carlo simulations, which attempt to give us a range of returns over time for the specific portfolios we have created.

Now it's time to look at all this information with real money. Some of you are novices, just beginning your investment path to becoming millionaires, and you have a relatively small amount of money. Others of you will have larger sums to invest. Some of you are young enough to contemplate investing over several decades, perhaps even 40 years. Others will not have that luxury of time. Our goal is to provide portfolios for each situation, along with different starting amounts, a continuing investing plan, and what you can expect as a return on your investment over the years, given different scenarios of future events.

Here are the three starting amounts that we will work with (which we first showed you in chapter 13). It's unlikely that one of these will match your personal investment amount exactly, so pick the one that comes closest.

- **Portfolio 1** has a starting amount of $10,000; it assumes monthly contributions of $200 for the first 5 years, then contributions of $400 a month for the following 5 years, and contributions of $550 a month for the remaining 30 years.

- **Portfolio 2** has a starting amount of $50,000; it assumes monthly contributions of $300 for the first 5 years, then contributions of $500 a month for the following 5 years, and contributions of $1,000 a month for the remaining 30 years.

- **Portfolio 3** has a starting amount of $120,000; it assumes monthly contributions of $750 for the first 5 years, then contributions of $1,200 a month for the following 5 years, and contributions of $1,500 a month for the remaining 30 years.

Now we put the results of these investment programs into the tables that follow. Table 15.1, which we showed you in chapter 13, applies to all three of the recommended portfolios. It displays the results of the Monte Carlo simulations for our recommended portfolio allocations. In this table, the results are expressed as percentage returns. Have a look at the numeric values in the table.

These values show the Monte Carlo anticipated returns, in numeric percentages, for our proposed investment based on the portfolios we have recommended, both the aggressive portfolio and the moderate portfolio. The table also displays the expected range of returns for 1, 5, 10, 20, 30, and 40 years.

Observe that the range of returns for the aggressive portfolio is wider than for the moderate portfolio. This makes sense. The aggressive portfolio will have higher potential gains and higher

TABLE 15.1: Monte Carlo Simulation: Return Forecast

| | Percentile | | | | |
	95th	75th	50th	25th	5th
1 Year					
Aggressive	37.55	18.09	7.32	-2.21	-15.16
Moderate	29.06	15.09	6.91	-0.77	-10.68
5 Year					
Aggressive	20.53	12.71	7.60	3.03	-3.12
Moderate	16.90	11.00	7.04	3.55	-1.26
10 Year					
Aggressive	16.65	11.30	7.82	4.42	-0.51
Moderate	13.78	9.84	7.23	4.61	0.94
20 Year					
Aggressive	13.75	10.20	7.71	5.35	2.20
Moderate	11.73	9.01	7.12	5.37	3.02
30 Year					
Aggressive	12.68	9.69	7.68	5.66	3.04
Moderate	10.95	8.63	7.11	5.61	3.59
40 Year					
Aggressive	12.02	9.33	7.60	5.93	3.44
Moderate	10.39	8.41	7.08	5.82	3.96

Source: Morningstar

potential losses than the moderate portfolio. Moreover, that range of returns in both portfolios will narrow over time. Indeed, over long periods of time, the returns will naturally drift closer to their historic averages. For example, the aggressive portfolio has an expected (or average) return of 7.32 percent. Note, however, that in any given year, the range of returns can go from a vertiginous high of 37.55 percent to a loss of 15.16 percent. A wide range of possibilities indeed. Now look at the range of returns for the same portfolio over 20 years. These returns would represent the average returns per year over a 20-year period. Now the high return expectation is 13.75 percent per year to a low of 2.20 percent per year.

Table 15.2 shows the dollar results of investing in Portfolio 1, which has a starting amount of $10,000 and a reinvestment

TABLE 15.2: Portfolio 1 ($10,000 Starting Amount)

			Percentile		
	95th	75th	50th	25th	5th
Aggressive					
1 Year	16,154.61	14,208.70	13,131.99	12,179.06	10,884.31
5 Year	44,228.65	33,773.65	28,436.37	24,272.21	19,409.02
10 Year	117,875.57	86,173.31	70,612.39	57,525.58	44,132.71
20 Year	506,740.90	328,563.37	245,076.48	184,810.70	131,087.93
30 Year	1,679,839.62	908,323.99	613,133.56	424,031.65	257,020.98
40 Year	4,832,904.00	2,226,847.30	1,381,223.30	848,935.81	445,627.54
Moderate					
1 Year	15,306.26	13,909.39	13,090.88	12,323.22	11,332.05
5 Year	38,962.18	31,777.88	27,910.80	24,774.71	20,894.78
10 Year	100,550.24	79,165.28	67,698.13	58,405.32	47,284.60
20 Year	397,852.06	283,593.51	228,296.33	185,050.46	140,958.90
30 Year	1,156,523.40	740,888.29	553,136.43	413,671.75	281,311.09
40 Year	2,981,002.47	1,681,966.78	1,199,704.88	830,713.73	509,490.87

Source: Morningstar

as indicated at the beginning of the chapter. The table shows the results for both the moderate investment strategy and the aggressive investment strategy. Young investors might choose the aggressive portfolio, since time will generally heal the bumps along the way. This has certainly been true in the past.

There's a lot of data in these tables, so don't rush through them. If you take the time to understand what they represent now, then when you come back to them, you'll know everything you need to know and where to look.

Again, remember that these returns are based on the initial investment of $10,000 and the ensuing monthly investments we indicated. Glance at the table of returns and you'll see the expected return (50th percentile) and the range of returns at the extremes. For example, in the aggressive portfolio, the 30-year expected (50th percentile) result for your portfolio is a value of $613,133.56. If you start young, and invest for 40 years, you are likely to have a portfolio valued at $1.38 million. Remember, these are estimates based on history, not a guarantee. But history is all we have to go on, and it is the best assurance we can get without a crystal ball.

The returns for the $50,000 starting portfolio and the $120,000 starting portfolio are shown in Table 15.3 and Table 15.4.

The numbers here get interesting, even a bit dizzying. In Portfolio 2 the expected result for the aggressive portfolio (50th percentile) is $1.3 million after 30 years. If you have 40 years to invest, the portfolio jumps to $2.9 million. The expected returns in Portfolio 3 are even more staggering: if this applies to you, have a look.

TABLE 15.3: Portfolio 2 ($50,000 Starting Amount)

			Percentile		
	95th	75th	50th	25th	5th
Aggressive					
1 Year	72,373.04	62,643.48	57,259.97	52,495.31	46,021.54
5 Year	156,093.33	114,085.39	93,543.56	77,235.53	59,632.71
10 Year	327,420.78	222,430.52	173,064.21	134,785.50	94,060.07
20 Year	1,232,210.79	747,537.61	538,006.19	369,926.06	273,073.19
30 Year	3,836,436.01	1,990,614.67	1,304,764.49	890,175.07	531,161.16
40 Year	10,739,962.14	4,806,716.81	2,931,233.68	1,788,091.66	910,562.40
Moderate					
1 Year	68,131.31	61,146.97	57,054.40	53,216.08	48,260.27
5 Year	135,579.82	106,284.11	91,007.30	78,784.92	64,615.63
10 Year	267,526.28	199,740.52	164,889.09	136,343.47	103,862.43
20 Year	928,506.37	637,739.85	496,385.81	395,260.62	295,183.02
30 Year	2,565,105.09	1,599,175.16	1,164,675.78	864,752.20	581,745.96
40 Year	6,602,491.45	3,592,906.96	2,515,056.30	1,723,374.49	1,022,976.76

Source: Morningstar

TABLE 15.4: Portfolio 3 ($120,000 Starting Amount)

| | \multicolumn{5}{c}{Percentile} | | | | |
	95th	75th	50th	25th	5th
Aggressive					
1 Year	174,055.30	150,704.35	137,783.93	126,348.74	110,811.71
5 Year	377,494.17	276,294.38	226,572.63	187,255.39	145,094.14
10 Year	791,263.81	537,736.18	418,624.49	325,837.38	227,386.26
20 Year	2,750,495.56	1,629,097.74	1,136,366.95	821,308.41	541,008.02
30 Year	8,312,701.81	4,138,149.62	2,631,315.45	1,760,817.44	1,012,899.71
40 Year	22,522,242.97	9,762,212.05	5,830,409.04	3,473,286.39	1,667,941.42
Moderate					
1 Year	163,875.15	147,112.72	137,290.55	128,078.58	116,184.65
5 Year	327,758.49	257,248.42	220,584.37	191,045.26	156,772.61
10 Year	647,070.21	483,131.06	398,640.90	329,693.33	251,193.20
20 Year	2,050,079.93	1,373,524.30	1,046,326.78	815,587.37	593,269.55
30 Year	5,466,056.18	3,271,752.79	2,346,947.28	1,716,357.01	1,116,348.53
40 Year	13,673,622.08	7,274,691.75	4,945,381.78	3,325,286.43	1,924,434.77

Source: Morningstar

How Realistic Is All This?

We know what you're thinking: this all sounds too good to be true. Indeed, as you may have asked earlier, "If it's this simple, why aren't more people rich?" If we had to sum it up in one word, that word would be "discipline." The sad reality is that most people don't save and invest with enough discipline and regularity—many don't have a dedicated plan like this that they follow religiously.

Another deterrent to great wealth is life. Life often puts financial demands on us that we have difficulty meeting. Your son's college tuition, or perhaps your daughter's wedding, may well take precedence over next year's monthly contributions to your investment portfolio. We need to be realistic about this. If there's a temporary interruption in your plans, don't let that deter you from staying the course and getting back on track as soon as you can. If you maintain discipline, a temporary interruption shouldn't derail your objectives. You'll get to that millionaire status anyway!

In the next chapter, we'll suggest specific funds and ETFs for your investment portfolio.

16

Populating
Your Portfolio

NOW COMES THE TIME to fill in the blanks and discuss real investment options to begin your journey toward your million-dollar portfolio. First, a word about this process: recommending specific investments in a book format has its perils. We aren't having a face-to-face discussion, so if something changes with one of these recommendations, we won't be readily available to answer your questions or suggest what to do. For example, if the performance of an actively managed fund deteriorates, that needs to be examined. Did the original manager leave? Is there some other explanation for the poor performance? For such reasons, most books do not offer specific recommendations. It would be next to impossible, however, for us to teach you how to use the 30-Minute Millionaire strategy without including concrete advice. We can't very well stop short of specific recommendations.

Furthermore, the vast majority of the recommendations are index funds. Index funds mirror the market, or their category, so they are not dependent on the skill of a particular manager who might decide to move or retire. It is highly unlikely that an external event sometime in the future would prompt a decision to get out of index funds. Note, too, that we are recommending up to three funds in each category from which to choose, using whatever characteristics matter most to you.

These portfolios will conform to the Monte Carlo projections in the preceding chapters. In doing so, they offer a realistic path to your future wealth. Use them in conjunction with one another. Remember that the Monte Carlo simulations will give you the expected returns through time for your portfolio, as well as the range of possible returns under different sets of circumstances.

The $10,000 portfolio looks different from the others simply because many of the funds we recommend have minimum starting amounts that cannot be met by the amount of money available in the $10,000 portfolio. We solved the size problem by finding ETFs that have characteristics similar to the funds we recommend in the larger portfolios. That said, as your portfolio grows over time, you may want to switch to one of the other funds. Before you do, check the performance of both and see if a switch makes sense. (This won't take much time out of your 30 minutes!)

For all portfolios, we have indicated our first choices of funds or ETFs that are readily available to buy through brokers where you are likely to open an account, such as Schwab or Fidelity. We are quite fond of Dimensional Fund Advisors (DFA) funds, and would have listed some of them first, except that to access DFA funds you need to open an account with a broker authorized to sell them, and there may be a fee involved.

Tables 16.1 through 16.3 on the following pages show recommended investments for each portfolio, followed by a listing of the funds and a description of each. For full information on these funds, consult each individual fund's prospectus.

Here's a brief description and the symbols of the suggested funds and ETFs. These summaries are adapted from the funds' own descriptions of their objectives:

DFA World ex US Government (DWFIX)

The World ex US Government Portfolio seeks its investment objective by investing in a universe of obligations issued primarily by non-US government issuers and supranational organizations, and their agencies, having investment grade credit ratings at the time of purchase. At the present time, Dimensional Fund Advisors LP (the "Advisor") expects that most investments will be made in the obligations of issuers determined by the Advisor to be associated with countries with developed markets. The Advisor selects the portfolio's foreign country and currency compositions based on an evaluation of various factors, including, but not limited to, relative interest rates and exchange rates. Generally, the World ex US Government Portfolio will purchase fixed income securities that mature between five and 15 years from the date of settlement. The portfolio may also enter into forward foreign currency contracts to attempt to protect against uncertainty in the level of future foreign currency rates; to hedge against fluctuations in currency exchange rates; or to transfer balances from one currency to another.

DFA US Small Cap Portfolio (DFSTX)

Using a market capitalization weighted approach, the US Small Cap Portfolio purchases a broad and diverse group of readily marketable US small-cap companies' securities. For purposes of the US Small Cap Portfolio, the Advisor considers small-cap companies to be companies whose market capitalizations are generally in the lowest 10 percent of total market capitalization, or companies whose market capitalizations are smaller than the 1,000th largest US company (whichever results in the higher market

TABLE 16.1: Recommended Allocation, Portfolio 1

$10,000 Portfolio				
	Aggressive Allocation	Moderate Allocation	Aggressive Investment	Moderate Investment
Small Cap Domestic	15%	10%	$1,500.00	$1,000.00
Large Cap Domestic	17%	20%	$1,700.00	$2,000.00
Domestic Fixed Income	8%	25%	$800.00	$2,500.00
Emerging Market	15%	10%	$1,500.00	$1,000.00
International Equity	14%	10%	$1,400.00	$1,000.00
Gold	3%	5%	$300.00	$500.00
Real Estate	10%	5%	$1,000.00	$500.00
International Sovereign Fixed Income	3%	5%	$300.00	$500.00
All Cap Alpha Manager	15%	10%	$1,500.00	$1,000.00

capitalization break). As of December. 31, 2014, the market capitalization of a small-cap company was $3.938 billion or below.

DFA Global Real Estate Securities (DFGEX)

The DFA Global Real Estate Securities Portfolio seeks to achieve exposure to a broad portfolio of US and non-US companies' securities in the real estate industry, with a focus on real estate investment trusts (REITs) or companies that Dimensional Fund Advisors LP considers to be REIT-like entities. The DFA Global Real Estate Securities Portfolio may pursue its investment objective by investing its assets in the DFA Real Estate Securities Portfolio, DFA International Real Estate Securities Portfolio (the

Recommended Investments, Portfolio 1		
$10,000 Portfolio		
Main Suggested Investment Vehicle	Alternative 1	Alternative 2
Vanguard Total Stock Market ETF		
Vanguard Total Stock Market ETF		
Ridge Worth Seix Core Bond Fund	Schwab Short-Term Bond Market Fund	
iShares MSCI Emerging Marketgs		
iShares MSCI EAFE ETF		
SPDR Gold Shares		
Vanguard REIT ETF		
SPDR Barclays International		
Eventide Gilead Fund	Delaware Select Growth Fund	

"Underlying Funds"), and/or directly in securities of companies in the real estate industry.

The DFA Global Real Estate Securities Portfolio and Underlying Funds generally consider a company to be principally engaged in the real estate industry if the company derives at least 50 percent of its revenue or profits from the ownership, management, development, construction, or sale of residential, commercial, industrial, or other real estate; has at least 50 percent of the value of its assets invested in residential, commercial, industrial, or other real estate; or is organized as a REIT or REIT-like entity. REIT and REIT-like entities are types of real estate companies that pool investors' funds for investment

TABLE 16.2: Recommended Allocation, Portfolio 2

$50,000 Portfolio				
	Aggressive Allocation	Moderate Allocation	Aggressive Investment	Moderate Investment
Small Cap Domestic	15%	10%	$7,500.00	$5,000.00
Large Cap Domestic	17%	20%	$8,500.00	$10,000.00
Domestic Fixed Income	8%	25%	$4,000.00	$12,500.00
Emerging Market	15%	10%	$7,500.00	$5,000.00
International Equity	14%	10%	$7,000.00	$5,000.00
Gold	3%	5%	$1,500.00	$2,500.00
Real Estate	10%	5%	$5,000.00	$2,500.00
International Sovereign Fixed Income	3%	5%	$1,500.00	$2,500.00
All Cap Alpha Manager	15%	10%	$7,500.00	$5,000.00

primarily in income-producing real estate or real estate related loans or interests.

SPDR® S&P 500 ETF Trust (SPY)
The SPDR S&P 500 ETF Trust seeks to provide investment results that, before expenses, correspond generally to the price and yield performance of the S&P 500 Index.

SPDR® Gold Shares (GLD)
The investment objective of the trust is for SPDR Gold Shares (GLD) to reflect the performance of the price of gold bullion, less the trust's expenses. SPDR Gold Shares represent fractional,

Recommended Investments, Portfolio 2

$50,000 Portfolio

Main Suggested Investment Vehicle	Alternative 1	Alternative 2
Fidelity Small Cap Enhanced	DFA US Small Cap Portfolio	Vanguard Russell 2000 Index
SPDR S&P 500 ETF Trust	Fidelity Large Cap Stock Fund	Vanguard 500 Index Fund
Vanguard Short-Term Bond Index	Fidelity Total Bond Fund	
Fidelity Total Emerging Market	DFA Emerging Markets Portfolio	Vanguard Emerging Markets
Vanguard International Growth	Fidelity Total International	iShares MSCI EAFE ETF
SPDR Gold Shares	Actual Gold	
Fidelity Real Estate Investment	DFA Global Real Estate Securities	Voya Real Estate Fund
Fidelity International Bond	DFA World ex US Government	
Akre Focus Fund	Lazard US Equity Concentrated	Causeway International Value

undivided beneficial ownership interests in the trust—the sole assets of which are gold bullion, and, from time to time, cash. SPDR Gold Shares are intended to lower a large number of the barriers preventing investors from using gold as an asset allocation and trading tool. These barriers have included the logistics of buying, storing, and insuring gold.

DFA Emerging Markets Portfolio (DFEMX)

The investment objective of the Emerging Markets Portfolio is to achieve long-term capital appreciation. The Emerging Markets Portfolio is a feeder portfolio and pursues its objective by substantially investing all of its assets in its corresponding master

TABLE 16.3: Recommended Allocation, Portfolio 3

	$120,000 Portfolio			
	Aggressive Allocation	Moderate Allocation	Aggressive Investment	Moderate Investment
Small Cap Domestic	15%	10%	$18,000.00	$12,000.00
Large Cap Domestic	17%	20%	$20,400.00	$24,000.00
Domestic Fixed Income	8%	25%	$9,600.00	$30,000.00
Emerging Market	15%	10%	$18,000.00	$12,000.00
International Equity	14%	10%	$16,800.00	$12,000.00
Gold	3%	5%	$3,600.00	$6,000.00
Real Estate	10%	5%	$12,000.00	$6,000.00
International Sovereign Fixed Income	3%	5%	$3,600.00	$6,000.00
All Cap Alpha Manager	15%	10%	$18,000.00	$12,000.00

fund (the Emerging Markets Series of The DFA Investment Trust Company), which has the same investment objective and policies as the portfolio.

Akre Focus Fund (AKRIX)

The goal at Akre Capital Management is to preserve and enhance client capital by creating investment portfolios characterized by low levels of business risk. Akre has met this goal with a direct approach of investing in businesses that, in their view, compound shareholder capital at above average rates of return.

Recommended Investments, Portfolio 3

$120,000 Portfolio

Main Suggested Investment Vehicle	Alternative 1	Alternative 2
Vanguard Total Stock Market ETF	DFA US Small Cap Portfolio	Vanguard Russell 2000 Index
Vanguard Total Stock Market ETF	Fidelity Large Cap Stock Fund	Vanguard 500 Index Fund
Ridge-Worth Seix Core Bond Fund	Fidelity Total Bond Fund	
iShares MSCI Emerging Marketgs	DFA Emerging Markets Portfolio	Vanguard Emerging Markets
iShares MSCI EAFE ETF	Fidelity Total International	iShares MSCI EAFE ETF
SPDR Gold Shares	Actual Gold	
Vanguard REIT ETF	DFA Global Real Estate Securities	Voya Real Estate Fund
SPDR Barclays International	DFA World ex US Government	
Eventide Gilead Fund	Lazard US Equity Concentrated	Causeway International Value

Vanguard International Growth (VWILX)

The fund invests in the stocks of companies located outside the United States. In selecting stocks, the fund's advisors evaluate foreign markets around the world and choose companies with above-average growth potential. The fund uses multiple investment advisors to manage its portfolio.

Vanguard Short-Term Bond Index (VBIRX)

The Vanguard Short-Term Bond Index Fund seeks to track the performance of a market-weighted bond index with a short-term dollar-weighted average maturity. The fund seeks to track the performance of the Barclays US 1–5 Year Government/Credit Float Adjusted Index.

Causeway International Value (CIVIX)

The Causeway International Value Fund's investment objective is to seek long-term growth of capital and income. The fund invests primarily in common stocks of companies located in developed countries outside the United States. Normally, the fund invests at least 80 percent of its total assets in stocks of companies located in at least 10 foreign countries and invests the majority of its total assets in companies that pay dividends or repurchase their shares.

SPDR® Barclays International (BWX)

The SPDR Barclays International Treasury Bond ETF seeks to provide investment results that, before fees and expenses, correspond generally to the price and yield performance of the Barclays Global Treasury Ex-US Capped Index.

Vanguard Total Stock Market ETF (VTI)

The Vanguard Total Stock Market ETF seeks to track the performance of the CRSP US Total Market Index. The fund employs a passively managed, index-sampling strategy, and its large-, mid-, and small-cap equities are diversified across growth and value styles.

iShares MSCI Emerging Markets (EEM)

The iShares MSCI Emerging Markets ETF seeks to track the investment results of an index composed of large- and mid-cap emerging market equities.

iShares MSCI EAFE ETF (EFA)

The iShares MSCI EAFE ETF seeks to track the investment results of an index composed of large- and mid-cap developed market equities, excluding the US and Canada.

Vanguard REIT ETF (VNQ)

The Vanguard REIT ETF invests in stocks issued by real estate investment trusts (REITs), companies that purchase office buildings, hotels, and other real property. The goal of the fund is to closely track the return of the MSCI US REIT Index, a gauge of real estate stocks.

Vanguard Russell 2000 Index Fund (VRTIX)

The Vanguard Russell 2000 Index Fund seeks to track the performance of the 2,000 smallest companies in the Russell 3000 Index.

Fidelity Large Cap Stock Fund (FLCSX)

The Fidelity Large Cap Stock Fund normally invests at least 80 percent of assets in common stocks of companies with large market capitalizations (companies with market capitalizations similar to companies in the Russell 1000 Index or the S&P 500). The fund invests in growth stocks, value stocks, or both.

Fidelity Total Emerging Market (FTEMX)

The Fidelity Total Emerging Market Fund seeks to take advantage of disparate opportunities between emerging-market debt and emerging-market equity across countries and regions. The fund normally invests approximately 60 percent of assets in stocks and other equity securities and places the remainder in bonds and other debt securities, including lower-quality debt securities, when its outlook is neutral.

Fidelity Real Estate Investment (FRESX)

The Fidelity Real Estate Investment Fund normally invests at least 80 percent of assets in securities of companies principally engaged in the real estate industry and other real estate related investments, primarily in common stocks.

Fidelity Total International (FTIEX)
The Fidelity Total International Fund normally invests primarily in non-US dollar-denominated securities, including securities of issuers located in emerging markets.

Voya Real Estate Fund (CRARX)
The Voya Real Estate Fund primarily invests in US REITs that own and manage commercial real estate with market capitalizations typically above $100 million at the time of purchase.

Fidelity Small Cap Enhanced Index Fund (FCPEX)
The Fidelity Small Cap Enhanced Index Fund normally invests at least 80 percent of assets in common stocks included in the Russell 2000 Index, which is a market capitalization-weighted index of companies with small market capitalizations. The fund generally uses computer-aided, quantitative analysis to select stocks that may have the potential to provide a higher total return than that of the Russell 2000 Index.

Fidelity Total Bond Fund (FTBFX)
The Fidelity Total Bond Fund normally invests at least 80 percent of assets in debt securities of all types and repurchase agreements for those securities. Using the Barclays US Universal Bond Index as a guide, the fund allocates assets across the investment-grade, high yield, and emerging market asset classes and invests up to 20 percent of assets in lower-quality debt securities. The fund is managed to have similar overall interest rate risk to the index and invests in domestic and foreign issuers, allocating assets across different asset classes, market sectors, and maturities.

To select investments, the fund analyzes the credit quality of the issuer; the issuer's potential for success; the credit, currency, and economic risks of the security and its issuer; security-specific features; current and potential future valuation; and trading opportunities. The fund also engages in transactions that have a leveraging effect, including investments in derivatives—such as swaps (interest rate, total return, and credit default), options, and futures contracts—and forward-settling securities, to adjust the fund's risk exposure. The fund invests in Fidelity's central funds (specialized investment vehicles used by Fidelity funds to invest in particular security types or investment disciplines).

Vanguard 500 Index Fund (VFIAX)
The Vanguard 500 Index Fund employs a passively managed, full-replication approach in seeking to track the performance of the S&P 500 Index with US large-cap equity diversified across growth and value styles. The fund remains fully invested at all times.

Vanguard Emerging Markets Stock Index Fund (VEMAX)
The Vanguard Emerging Markets Stock Index Fund seeks to track the performance of a benchmark index, the FTSE Emerging Market Index, which measures the investment return of stocks issued by companies located in emerging market countries.

Lazard US Equity Concentrated (LEVIX)
The Lazard US Equity Concentrated Portfolio is a concentrated, all-cap fund that seeks long-term capital appreciation. It is benchmark agnostic, seeking to outperform any broad based market benchmark (i.e., S&P 500 Index, Russell 1000 Index, Russell 3000 Index) by taking advantage of valuation anomalies and investing in companies that compound earnings and capital. The portfolio invests in financially productive companies across the market capitalization spectrum, employing intensive fundamental analysis and accounting validation to identify investment opportunities. The portfolio typically invests in 15 to 35 companies with market capitalizations generally greater than $350 million.

Eventide Gilead Fund (ETGLX)

The Eventide Gilead Fund is a diversified mutual fund that seeks to provide long-term capital appreciation. The fund invests in primarily equity securities of companies that demonstrate values and business practices that are ethical and sustainable while providing an attractive investment opportunity. The fund also invests in securities that have significant near-term appreciation potential.

Delaware Select Growth Fund (DVEAX)

The Delaware Select Growth Fund invests in companies of any size or market capitalization that its portfolio managers believe have long-term capital appreciation potential and are expected to grow faster than the US economy.

RidgeWorth Seix Core Bond Fund (STIGX)

The RidgeWorth Seix Core Bond Fund seeks total return (comprised of capital appreciation and income) that consistently exceeds the total return of the broad US dollar-denominated, investment grade market of intermediate-term government and corporate bonds.

Schwab Short-Term Bond Market (SWBDX)

The investment seeks high current income by tracking the performance of the Barclays US Government/Credit 1–5 Year Index. The fund primarily invests in a diversified portfolio of debt instruments designed to track the performance of the index. It uses the index as a guide in structuring the fund's portfolio and selecting its investments. The fund normally invests at least 80 percent of its net assets in debt instruments of varying maturities. It invests primarily in investment grade instruments. The fund may invest in fixed-, variable-, or floating-rate debt instruments. It also may invest in debt instruments of domestic and foreign issuers.

Rebalancing

Over the coming years, your different asset classes will inevitably grow at different rates—and that's good. The last thing you want to experience is all of your investments going up and down at the same time. Avoiding this vertiginous and stomach-turning type of volatility is the very purpose of asset allocation. So this means that over time, your fastest-growing investments will account for more than their initial percentage allocation of your portfolio, and your slowest-growing investments will wind up below their initial allocations. Periodic rebalancing of your holdings will solve this conundrum.

For example, what should you do if your original allocation to large-cap stocks was 25 percent, but as a result of stock markets going up, your large-cap stocks now account for 32 percent of your portfolio? The answer is to "rebalance"—sell some of your large-cap funds to bring them back to 25 percent of your portfolio, then use the proceeds to add to the allocations that have performed less well (and are now below their original allocation percentages).

You're probably wondering how often you need to rebalance. We wish there was a definitive answer. This subject is one of the most debated topics among investment professionals, so whatever we suggest, you can assume some others will have a different point of view. For some, rebalancing too often is a process in which you punish your best performing assets by selling a portion of them in order to add to, or reward, your worst performing assets. Indeed, that is precisely what rebalancing does. If your stocks are going up, what's the hurry to sell? Wouldn't you want to hang on to your winners?

The main argument for rebalancing is that the original asset allocation you chose was based on a thoughtful analysis of the risk and rewards of the different asset classes and the appropriate percentage of each to own. If they get out of line, your portfolio is no longer the same one you started with. You wouldn't, however, want to rebalance every week. There is validity to the notion of letting your winners run for a while, so our contention is that rebalancing should occur about once a year or so. If an asset class gets seriously out of line, you may want to rebalance more often to get it back in line. Let's say your small-cap fund, which had an initial allocation of 15 percent of your holdings, has a terrific run and now accounts for not 15 percent, but 22 percent of your portfolio. You should probably rebalance, because small caps are historically volatile, and if you let that allocation get too large, you will have a correspondingly riskier portfolio than you bargained for.

Here are some guidelines: rebalance your portfolio once a year, or whenever a particular allocation has become more than 25 percent higher than in your original plan. For example, if your original small-cap allocation was 15 percent, once the allocation rises to 19 percent or 20 percent, you should rebalance back to 15 percent.

What about Your Own Ideas about Your Portfolio?

We assume you're not an expert in finance and the stock market—after all, that's why you're reading this book—but that doesn't mean you don't have your own views of the world, the future, and some insight into the investment process. There will inevitably be occasions when you have an idea you feel strongly about and that you want to include in your investment plan. Go ahead!

But with some limits.

For example, let's say inflation is on the rise and you want to increase your allocation to include gold. You might want to take some money out of stocks or bonds, or perhaps your real estate investments, and add gold holdings. The only limit you should consider is to not throw off the allocations discussed earlier. The projections to get you to the million-dollar mark were based on probabilities inherent in the allocations we suggested. So deviate if you wish, we encourage you to follow your own good instincts, but do so within limits.

You shouldn't, however, deviate from the allocations by more than 10 percent. For example, if a recommended allocation to a specific asset class is 25 percent, don't increase it to more than 35 percent, or decrease it to under 15 percent. While these changes may affect the long-term outcome, if your instincts are correct, you could do even better. Honestly, we'd prefer that you stick to the allocations we recommend since there is solid historical evidence that they will get you to where you want to be. But, human nature being what it is, we thought it important to address the circumstances in which you would want to make your own choices for at least part of your holdings. And as we said, who knows, you may be right!

17

Do I Need an Advisor?

BEFORE ADDRESSING THIS IMPORTANT question, remember that one of us (Peter) is affiliated with an investment-consulting firm. So keep that in mind when considering the advice we give. That said, we're trying to be scrupulously objective with our thoughts on this subject. Judge for yourself.

In the beginning of your investment program, when you don't have much money to invest, you are likely better off following the advice in this book and doing it on your own. Sadly, that's because of how investment advisors and brokers work. Since your portfolio is small, few professional advisors will be willing to take you on as a client.

There are a number of online investment programs that charge small fees for what is basically automated advice. These portfolios tend to be one-size-fits-all. There will be little opportunity with these programs for you to customize your investments according to your chosen allocation and your personal preferences.

Later on, when your portfolio has increased in value, you may want to get some professional advice. Indeed, when you reach the stage of a million-dollar portfolio, you will be able to attract a high level of investment advice from those advisors who deal only with larger investment accounts. When that happy day arrives, pick up this book again and read what follows.

Investment Advisors Are Not All the Same

Back when your parents and grandparents were investing, they generally dealt with stockbrokers for all of their investment needs. In the 1920s and 1930s, stockbrokers were called "customers' men." (There weren't any women in the field yet.) Today, there is no limit to the creativity of investment advisor titles. You see, the once honorable title of "stockbroker" has been largely swept to the sidelines, the result of too many scandals involving unscrupulous securities salesmen over the years. (Did you see the film *The Wolf of Wall Street*?) As of this writing, there are two standards of investment advice offered to clients. Your advisor will adhere to one or the other, though one is much better than the other. We'll explain.

Registered Investment Advisors (RIAs) adhere to what is known as the "fiduciary standard." This standard requires the advisor to put the client's interests first. The lesser standard is the "suitability standard," which says that the advisor can recommend investment products to the client so long as the investment is deemed suitable for the client's goals, risk tolerance, and objectives. There is an important distinction here. In the latter case, there might be two different funds to recommend to the client that are similar, but one of them pays the broker a fat commission and the other doesn't. The broker will be tempted to sell the client the one with the big commission, because the investment is "suitable." An RIA who adheres to the fiduciary standard wouldn't be able to do that.

Most brokers adhere to the lesser suitability standard, whereas RIAs adhere to the fiduciary standard. Obviously, brokers make more money selling high-margin products, and the brokerage and insurance industries have been fighting to preserve this lesser standard. There are currently no regulatory rules requiring all investment professionals to meet the fiduciary standard. (The debate over this lack of regulation continues in Congress.)

Don't get us wrong: there are many scrupulous brokers governed by the suitability standard who are honest advocates for their clients and who provide excellent service at a reasonable fee. If you find one, you're in luck. We would advise you, however, to opt for an advisor who adheres to the higher fiduciary standard.

Alphabet Soup

Another issue of interest is an advisor's qualifications. There have been a lot of creative qualifications dreamed up over the years. Some large firms even have their own, designed to impress you. Often, these professionals put their qualifications on business cards in the form of impressive initials that follow their name.

For your purposes, there are only two you should look for. They are:

1. Chartered Financial Analyst (CFA)

2. Certified Financial Planner (CFP)

Of the two certifications, the Chartered Financial Analyst is more difficult to receive. The CFA requires three years of study, and exams at each of three levels, before an advisor can qualify to put those initials on a business card. These individuals are well versed in finance theory, ethical practices, and a variety of complex investment tools. The Chartered Financial Planner focuses primarily on individual investors who want more than investment advice and who seek help planning their budgets, allocating their financial resources, and creating an investment plan.

Your personal interests and objectives will dictate which of the two you use. And let us add that there are plenty of qualified advisors who don't have any titles. If you're leaning toward working with an advisor who doesn't have either certification, you should ask for references from at least two clients of the particular advisor.

How Much Will Professional Advice Cost?

If you thought pricing and bargaining for a new car was complicated, welcome to the pricing ordeal for financial services. In an attempt to keep this simple, we'll break down the pricing formulas for investment services into three categories.

1. ASSET-BASED PRICING

Money managers and investment consultants often charge a fee based on the size of your assets. For accounts sized in the millions, the fee can vary from a high of 1 percent to a fraction of 1 percent. For a relatively small account, say $200,000, the fee might be 60 basis points, or 0.60 percent of the value of your investments (in this case, $1,200 a year). In the case of a money manager, what you're getting for this fee is the management of a portion of your portfolio by someone who likely specializes in a sector of the market (small cap, large cap, international, etc.). In the case of an investment consultant, the fee will likely be lower. Remember, however, that you pay a consultant for advice on asset allocation and manager selection and monitoring—this fee will be in addition to the fees you pay to the underlying managers.

2. HOURLY PRICING

Some advisors who help with asset allocation and manager or fund selection charge an hourly fee. They will also help write an investment policy for you to follow and be available for further consultation on your investments when you feel you need it.

3. FREE ADVICE!

Most brokers, who now go by more distinguished names such as "financial advisors," will proudly tell you that they do not charge a fee for their services. You have probably guessed that using these professionals will end up costing you the most money. Brokers are likely to be subject to the suitability rule, not the higher fiduciary standard, so they make their money on commissions they earn on the various products they sell. Need we say more?

If you are reading this chapter, in fact, it's quite possible you have now built up a significant portfolio and are ready to have some extra, professional eyes take a look at it. Then again, you may be content to continue managing your own investments. Whether you choose to work with a professional or continue investing on your own, make sure your decision matches your personality, history, and financial needs.

18

How to Spend Your 30 Minutes a Week

ONCE YOU HAVE FINISHED reading this book, you'll want to put into practice everything we've said about becoming a millionaire through managing your investments in only 30 minutes a week. As we discussed in earlier chapters, you will have already invested several hours to get to this point. You now understand the key principles of investing that will serve to get you to the millionaire status you strive to achieve. Let's sum up the main points.

- Stocks will be the engine of growth in your portfolio.

- You will own stocks in many different categories, including large and small US companies, as well as in Europe and other developed countries. You'll own stocks in emerging markets, too.

- You will emphasize passive funds, with a small exposure to active managers. History shows that it is very difficult to beat the market, so we advise foregoing the risk of underperformance by sticking with funds that give you consistent market performance.

- You understand the importance of diversification. Your portfolio will be intelligently diversified to smooth out any of the violent ups and downs of the market.

- Your portfolio will include non-correlated asset classes to contribute to your intelligent diversification. Gold will be one such asset class.

- You will not be tempted to buy individual stocks. You understand that picking stocks, like brain surgery, should be a full-time job. You'll let the pros pick the stocks for you.

- You won't waste time trying to outguess the market or listening to pundits who claim to know where the market is headed.

- Finally, you will be comfortable knowing that spending too much time on your investments will be counterproductive. You will spend just 30 minutes a week supervising your portfolio and making intelligent decisions for adjustments along the way.

30 Minutes a Week: A Checklist

There are a number of items you'll need to check, and adjustments you'll need to make, to keep your portfolio on track in the future. Some items on your checklist will occur at different intervals than others, so how you allot your 30 minutes a week will vary over time.

Here are the items you'll need to check, along with the frequency of attention for each item. Following the table, we'll describe in detail what you will be looking for and what your goals will be for each item in these weekly sessions.

TABLE 18.1: 30-Minute Checklist	
Activity	Frequency
Portfolio Total Value	Weekly
Portfolio Performance Versus Benchmark	Weekly
Manager Performance Versus Benchmark	Monthly
Check Status of Fund Manager	Monthly
Check Fees	Monthly
Allocate Your Monthly Cash Additions to Your Portfolio	Monthly
Rebalance Portfolio Holdings	Annually

PORTFOLIO TOTAL VALUE

Most likely, your brokerage statement will be accessible online so you'll be able to see the total value of your holdings whenever you'd like. You should review this statement once a week to check the value of your holdings. As your portfolio grows, you'll develop a sense of accomplishment when you see what you have created.

PORTFOLIO PERFORMANCE VERSUS BENCHMARK

The majority of your holdings will be in index funds, so a particular fund's performance should be almost identical to the benchmark. If there's a variance in performance, ask why. If a fund underperforms its benchmark over two to four quarters, consider a different fund in the same category.

MANAGER PERFORMANCE VERSUS BENCHMARK

For active managers, the benchmark comparison is even more important, but you may need to exercise patience. Outperformance is not, of course, a problem. Underperformance is. If a manager underperforms for six to twelve months, consider replacing that fund.

CHECK STATUS OF FUND MANAGER

This won't be necessary for most index funds, since they are designed to mirror their index performance. But for active funds, you want to be sure that the fund manager, the one who managed the fund when you first bought it, is still there. It's likely you bought the fund because of a particular manager's excellent performance, so if there's a change, you need to know about it and take action. In most cases, you'll want to sell the fund if the manager changes and replace it with a similar fund with a good performance record. Morningstar, which tracks mutual funds, is a good source of information.

CHECK FEES

Index fund fees are generally very low, often as low as 0.10 percent. Active management fees are considerably higher, and what you're paying for to justify the higher cost is a manager's skill. If managers are not beating the benchmark of their funds over time, then they're not earning their fees. Check to see that the fees are being earned and make certain that they haven't crept up and are no longer competitive. When checking fees, make sure you do an apples-to-apples comparison. Fees vary by type of asset class. Generally, emerging market fees are the highest and fees for bond funds are the lowest. And, of course, active management fees are always higher than passive management (index) fees. Your fund prospectus will list the fees.

ALLOCATE YOUR MONTHLY CASH ADDITIONS TO YOUR PORTFOLIO

As part of your 30-Minute Millionaire plan, you'll add funds to your portfolio every month. Ideally, you should add your funds proportionately to each fund, or manager, you own. This may not be practical early on, however, while your holdings are relatively small. Instead, consider adding to only one or two holdings each month and to the others in subsequent months. Over a long period of time, this action will have a negligible effect on your overall performance, compared to adding all the funds proportionally each month at the same time.

REBALANCE PORTFOLIO HOLDINGS

This will be tricky and will take up all of your 30 minutes, perhaps exceeding them. Since this rarely happens, however, that's OK. Some weeks you'll use less than 30 minutes to check on you portfolio. It will all average out.

Rebalancing needs to be done only once a year or, as we described earlier, whenever a particular asset class gets too large or small. Over time, not all of your holdings will grow at the same rate. Indeed, that's what we want, and that is the principle of diversification. As some holdings grow while others stagnate, your initial allocations will be affected. Here's an example: let's say you start out with 20 percent of your portfolio in large-cap stocks, perhaps through an S&P 500 index fund. If the index goes up faster than most other sectors of your portfolio, your allocation to this index fund may now account for 25 percent of your holdings. What do you do? You rebalance. You should sell 5 percent of your index holdings, then sprinkle the proceeds around the other holdings that haven't done as well to bring them back to their original starting allocation.

It's also useful to consider all the things you won't do in your allotted 30 minutes a week. You won't listen to the prognosticators who are worried that the market is overvalued or are screaming to buy. Sometimes they'll be right and sometimes they'll be wrong. You won't care. Whatever happens in the short term will not affect your long-term plan.

You won't worry about reading gobs of research reports on individual stocks, since you'll be paying someone to do that for you, and for most of your portfolio you'll be happy owning the entire market or whole sectors through index funds. You won't fret over how to time the market. You'll invest regularly, each month, as the funds allocated to your portfolio come in and get added to your holdings.

Now that we have mastered the strategy to becoming a 30-Minute Millionaire, we send you our best wishes for your future investing. We leave you with a practical, relatively simple-to-follow plan to build your fortune. We are confident that as you put our advice to practice, you will be on the path to success. We'll be cheering you on!

Notes

Chapter 2

1. Michelle Fox, "Here's how a janitor amassed an $8M fortune," CNBC.com (February 9, 2015): http://www.cnbc.com/2015/02/09/heres-how-a-janitor-amassed-an-8m-fortune.html.

Chapter 4

1. "20 savings mistakes people make," Bankrate.com (August 20, 2010): http://www.bankrate.com/finance/savings/20-savings-mistakes-that-people-make-1.aspx.

2. Ibid.

3. Michelle Fox, "Here's how a janitor amassed an $8M fortune," CNBC.com (February 9, 2015): http://www.

cnbc.com/2015/02/09/heres-how-a-janitor-amassed-an
-8m-fortune.html.

Chapter 5

1.	Lawrence Delevingne, "Cooperman bullish despite loss,"
	CNBC.com (February 10, 2015): http://www.cnbc.com/
	id/102414027.

2.	Ibid.

3.	Fred Imbert, "Warren Buffett's advice to LeBron
	James," CNBC.com (March 2, 2015): http://www.cnbc.
	com/2015/03/02/warren-buffetts-advice-to-lebron-james
	.html.

4.	PNC Financial Services Group, Inc., "Pensées: Active
	versus Passive," *PNC Investment Outlook* (March 2015).

Chapter 6

1.	Charles Rotblut, CFA and John C. Bogle, "Achieving
	Greater Long-Term Wealth Through Index Funds," *The
	AAII Journal* (June 2014): http://www.aaii.com/journal/
	article/achieving-greater-long-term-wealth-through
	-index-funds.touch.

2.	Tim Parker, "Jack Bogle Doesn't Think You Should Get
	Cozy With ETFs," Investopedia.com (February 12, 2013):
	http://www.investopedia.com/stock-analysis/2013/jack-
	bogle-doesnt-think-you-should-get-cozy-with-etfs-xlf
	-vnm-spxl0214.aspx.

3.	ETF.com Staff, "ETF League Table As Of May 22, 2015,"
	ETF.com (May 26, 2015): http://www.etf.com/sections/
	etf-league-tables/etf-league-table-may-22-2015.

4.	Myles Udland, "Jack Bogle: Only An Idiot Would
	Trade The S&P 500 All Day Long," Business Insider
	(September 22, 2014): http://www.businessinsider.com/

jack-bogle-and-cliff-asness-at-bloomberg-markets
-summit-2014-9.

Chapter 7

1. Matt Phillips, "Buffett's Buddy Charlie Munger to
    Goldbugs: 'You're A Jerk'," *The Wall Street Journal*,
    MarketBeat (January 12, 2011): http://blogs.wsj.com/
    marketbeat/2011/01/12/warren-buffett-bud-charlie
    -munger-to-goldbugs-youre-a-jerk/.

2. Ibid.

3. World Gold Council, "Central Banks," Gold.org (2015):
    http://www.gold.org/supply-and-demand/demand/
    central-banks.

Chapter 8

1. "Warren Buffett," Wikiquote.org (October, 2015): https://
    en.wikiquote.org/wiki/Warren_Buffett

2. Warren Buffett, "Buy American. I Am." *New York Times*
    (October 16, 2008): http://www.nytimes.com/2008/10/17/
    opinion/17buffett.html?_r=0.

3. Ibid.

4. Ibid.

Chapter 9

1. Aswath Damodaran, "Annual Returns on Stock, T. Bonds
    and T. Bills: 1928–Current," NYU Stern School of Business
    (January 5, 2015): http://pages.stern.nyu.edu/~adamodar/
    New_Home_Page/datafile/histretSP.html.

2. The World Bank Group, "GDP growth (annual %)," The
    World Bank: Data (2015): http://data.worldbank.org/
    indicator/NY.GDP.MKTP.KD.ZG.

3. Federal Reserve Bank of St. Louis, "Personal Saving Rate 2015-09," Economic Research: Federal Reserve Bank of St. Louis (September 2015): https://research.stlouisfed.org/fred2/series/PSAVERT.

4. Ben S. Bernanke, "At the Federal Reserve Bank of Kansas City Economic Symposium, Jackson Hole, Wyoming," Board of Governors of the Federal Reserve System (August 27, 2010): http://www.federalreserve.gov/newsevents/speech/bernanke20100827a.htm.

5. Tobias M. Levkovich and Lorraine M. Schmitt, "A Chart Worthy of Consideration," Citigroup (April 8, 2015).

6. Federal Reserve Bank of St. Louis, "Real Gross Private Domestic Investment 2014," Economic Research: Federal Reserve Bank of St. Louis (July 2015): https://research.stlouisfed.org/fred2/series/A006RL1A225NBEA.

7. Securities Industry and Financial Markets Association, "Statistics," sifma.org (2015): http://www.sifma.org/research/statistics.aspx.